To Nadia

MICHEL ROUX Jr

A life in the kitchen

Happy Kitchens!

MICHEL ROUX Jr

A life in the kitchen

WEIDENFELD & NICOLSON

First published in Great Britain in 2009
by Weidenfeld & Nicolson
10 9 8 7 6 5 4 3 2 1

Photography by Cristian Barnett
Cover, 38, 223, 297 (top right): Jon Wyand
Other photographs: see page 319

A CIP catalogue record for this book is available from the British Library.
ISBN-13: 978 0 297 84482 2

The Orion Publishing Group's policy is to use papers that are natural,
renewable and recyclable products and made from wood grown in sustainable
forests. The logging and manufacturing processes are expected to conform
to the environmental regulations of the country of origin.

Design director Lucie Stericker
Editorial director Susan Haynes
Designed by Smith & Gilmour
Calligraphy by Peter Horridge
Edited by Jinny Johnson
Index by Elizabeth Wiggans

Printed in Italy

Weidenfeld & Nicolson

The Orion Publishing Group Ltd
Orion House
5 Upper St Martin's Lane
London WC2H 9EA

www.orionbooks.co.uk

To Gisele and Emily, the two people
I most love cooking for

Contents

List of recipes 8

ONE

A taste of childhood 12
I had an idyllic childhood and I remember that life in our family always centred round food. I have happy memories of my parents bickering good-naturedly in the kitchen, always about what they were cooking. The ultimate goal was perfection. My father and my uncle would have furious arguments over how to make an omelette. Uncle Michel likes them with a bit of colour; my father says no colour. Both versions are delicious.

Michel on:
Roasts 21

TWO

Being a Roux 54
When I was growing up I wasn't really aware that my father and my uncle were so famous and that the name of Roux had become synonymous with everything to do with the finest of French food. The early days of Le Gavroche were hard work and I remember my mother making weekly trips to Paris to buy the best of ingredients for the restaurant. But we had lots of fun too, with some great fishing expeditions and wonderful holidays.

Michel on:
Cooking fresh fish 66

THREE

The masters' apprentice 76
I genuinely think I couldn't have done anything else. The only choice was when. At 16, I went to Paris to start my apprenticeship under Maître Pâtissier Hellegouarche, the finest pastry chef in France. Pastry making instills discipline – it's a science, unlike cooking, which can involve more than a bit of flair. I then moved to Alain Chapel's three-star restaurant near Lyon – the place where every young chef dreamed of working.

Michel on:
Cooking with spices and chillies 102
Salads 110
Offal 116

The Socialists under François Mitterand knew how to party and they wanted to show off the best France had to offer. As a National Service conscript in the kitchen at the Elysée Palace, I learned the classic French dishes – *maison bourgeoise*. The banquets were run like a military operation and the President checked all the menus and chose the wine. I was in charge of breakfast for President Mitterand – he had a gargantuan appetite.

Back in London after work experience at the Mandarin Hotel in Hong Kong I began to find my feet as a manager in the family businesses – Gavvers, Le Gamin, Le Poulbot and contract and private catering. There is huge tension in a Michelin-starred kitchen and a lot of pressure. Chefs work hard and play hard. The life is steamy and passionate and the amount of sexual innuendo – and sex – that goes on in a restaurant is incredible.

My wife Gisele is as passionate about food as I am. She was a manageress at one of our restaurants when we met. Her family, from the Cévennes region, really enjoy their food and hunt, fish and eat in the traditional way. Together with our daughter Emily we eat simply at home, but we take our time and enjoy our meals for what they are. A simple meal can be just as rewarding as a meal in a two- or three-star restaurant.

When I took over at Le Gavroche in 1991 I didn't fully realise what it signified and how people saw my father and uncle. Wherever you go in the world, the Roux name is like a gold standard in the industry. Most of the top names have been at Le Gavroche to learn. For the first few years I changed nothing, then gradually I started introducing my own style – still French, still classical, but with a lighter, more modern approach.

List of recipes

A taste of childhood

I was almost born in the kitchen. My mother actually went into labour as she was helping my father to cook, and she had to be rushed into hospital for my birth. My parents, Albert and Monique, had arrived in England from Paris in 1959 and I was born a year later. So not only was I born in England, I was also made in England. My parents were passionate fishermen and they always tell me that I was conceived during one of their fishing trips. Perhaps this explains my love of seafood – and of fishing?

My father had come to England to work as a private chef for Peter and Zara Cazalet. The Cazalets were well known in the racing world. In fact, they were trainers to the Queen Mother. They lived on a large estate called Fairlawne in Shipbourne, Kent. The estate still exists, but these days it's owned by another family. With my father's job came a wonderful pink house which was perhaps two or three miles away from Fairlawne. There was a big lawn in the front of the house with a cherry tree, and at the back was a small vegetable garden and a shed that my father used for keeping the rabbits and pigeons he reared for our table.

My earliest memories are of crawling around the kitchen of Fairlawne. To a toddler it appeared huge – a very, very big room with a great wooden table in the middle and tiles all around. I remember my father rolling pasta by hand on the table while I played underneath it. I used to play with little pieces of dough and eat them raw.

I remember that the kitchen always smelled of food. One of the first smells I remember is sugar – that very particular smell of caramelising sugar, sweet and sharp at the same time, completely unforgettable and absolutely mouthwatering. Certain smells and noises never leave you and that's one of them. My uncle Michel used to practise his sugar work in the kitchen at Fairlawne.

ABOVE LEFT: Fairlawne.
ABOVE RIGHT: Our house,
two or three miles away.

He'd come over to live in England soon after we arrived and he was working as a private chef for the Rothschild family.

One of the first tasks my father gave me as a child was churning the ice cream. There were no machines for this job then. Everything was done by hand and it was a very laborious process. I was five or maybe six years old and I remember it distinctly. There was a wooden bucket with a mechanical cylinder that was clasped into it and a wooden handle. You put in the ice and some rock salt, and the creamy mixture went in a separate container with a paddle you had to turn by hand. It made an amazing cracking sound as the ice was churned. The handle was so hard to turn and it took all my strength just to try to move it. I remember having tears in my eyes from the pain of trying to churn the ice and finally having to admit to defeat and give up the task.

My mother was always in the kitchen, too, either cooking for us or helping my father in the kitchen at the main house. We always had good and wholesome food and it was always eaten with the family. No matter how busy my parents were, we sat down and had a proper meal as a family.

And my father was very busy. It was a big house and the Cazalets often had lots of people staying at weekends. The Queen Mother used to come and visit the stables, and sometimes she stayed at the house. It was quite something for my father, who had very little money, to be cooking for the Queen Mother and to have his own house on the estate.

When my parents were too busy to watch over me, I was sent upstairs to stay with Mrs Bradbrook, the housekeeper. She always gave me an apple before I went to bed. I particularly remember her wonderful sponge puddings and hot chocolate. I can still almost taste them. Fairlawne was a very upstairs-downstairs sort of house, and Mr Bradbrook was the butler. I remember him clearly. He had a big bellowing voice and was quite portly, with rosy cheeks.

As far back as I can remember, family and food were the most important things in our lives. My sister Danielle and I were always encouraged to taste everything on the table. I remember first eating Camembert at the age of about three – creamy and salty all at once with that wonderful delicate casing.

It was the most glorious life for a child, complete paradise. My father was passionate about growing his own vegetables – he still is. And he cared for his animals very well, very carefully. The pigeons and the rabbits would eat out of his hand. My father had a great love and respect for his animals. It was of paramount importance to him that they had a proper life, were fed well and treated kindly. He would never tolerate cruelty to any animal. He made sure they had the best life possible. And then he gave them the chop.

After we settled in Fairlawne, my father's mother, Germaine, came over from France to live with us and she worked in the house as lady's maid to Zara Cazalet. I remember Mrs Cazalet screaming, 'Germaine!' and my grandmother would scuttle up the hall to find out what she wanted. My grandmother was not an easy woman, but she'd had to be tough because she'd brought up four children on her own and her life was hard. I never knew my grandfather, but apparently he drank and gambled, and then abandoned his family to live in North Africa. So my grandmother was left to manage with very little money.

Difficulty aside, my grandmother was an amazing character. I remember her standing in front of the fire, lifting her skirt up

CLOCKWISE FROM TOP LEFT: Helping out in our vegetable garden at Fairlawne in Kent. Playing with my father's rabbits. Me with my grandmother Germaine. With the rabbits again. Digging the garden becomes too much for me. Lunch in the garden with my cousin Dominique.

to warm herself. She'd flap her skirt up and down to warm her backside and she didn't care who saw her. She could be so crotchety and horrible, but she could be wonderful too. I remember some fabulous times with her, such as when we walked Zara Cazalet's dogs – they were little pugs which snuffled about. It was one of my grandmother's duties to walk the dogs and she used to take me with her. We would find wild strawberries in the hedgerows and gorge ourselves on them. You can't find proper wild strawberries any more. And in the winter we'd go into the woods to walk and collect chestnuts which we would roast at home.

It was the best childhood imaginable. We had such a lot of fun. Everything revolved around the family and it was a wonderful time. The house we lived in was big enough for all the family to come and visit from France as often as they could. My aunties, Martine and Liliane, came and they always brought food with them – cheese or sausage or wine. The things they brought were impossible to get in England at that time, so we fell upon these offerings as if they were precious treasures. And they were to us. Food was the most important thing in our house. It still is.

I always knew that my father was a professional chef and that cooking was what he did to earn his living. But my mother was always cooking as well. She would help my father in the kitchen at Fairlawne, of course. At home she was the main cook, but often they would cook together or he would give instructions to her about how he wanted things cooked. And he would get upset if it didn't turn out the way he wanted it.

My mother is a fantastic cook. She has a wonderful palate and is just as passionate about food as my father. But sometimes they disagreed on exactly how things should taste – about a sauce or how long a piece of meat should roast. They would bicker jokingly about things and how they should be. Although my father was the professional and my mother was the kitchen help, he would always ask her opinion. He would listen to her because he certainly respected her point of view and her palate. In our family we were always striving for the best food we could produce, both at home

CLOCKWISE FROM TOP LEFT: My father in the kitchen at Fairlawne. Me with my first cooker! Dad, at the stove again. And my father showing off his catch.

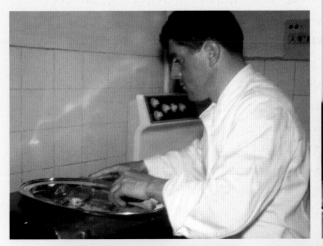

and at work. We were always interested in how to achieve that, how to get the ultimate end product. We all recognised good and bad – we are very much peas out of the same pod.

So I remember some arguments, but more than that I remember the food. We had lots of roasts, big hunks of meat, and game which was brought to the table on an enormous platter, and I remember as a child picking the meat from the bones of pheasant and guinea fowl. There is nothing like the smell of roasting meat, the smell from the caramelising of the fat and juices.

We never had to speak about the importance of food. It went without saying it was the most important thing in our lives. We took that for granted. Even now, the majority of the conversation when we sit down for lunch or dinner is about food, what we're eating now and what we'll eat for the next meal. It's in the family. We're always talking about food.

You have to remember that when my parents first came to England the only place you could buy olive oil was from the chemist, for unblocking your ears. A little while after that you could buy it at speciality shops, but it was very expensive. So every time someone went to France, they would bring something back – cheese, sausage, wine, olive oil. Sometimes we held our breath at customs, but no one ever came from France empty handed.

I remember my father saying to me from quite an early age, 'You must try this wine.' Certain wines stick in your memory because they have such a distinctive taste. Fine clarets, for example, have a deep oakiness that is so different from a fruity Beaujolais. And he would explain to me what made a good Beaujolais and how it was different from a claret. As children, we never had watered-down wine. We were always given just a little in a glass to try and always with meals.

Roasts

A roast is probably most people's favourite meal. I'm sure any poll would show that. I think it's because it's associated with family and friends sitting down together. You don't cook a roast for one. By its very nature, a roast is a meal for many. And there is the ceremony of bringing the bird or joint to the table. It's special, like a Japanese tea ceremony. The head of the house should carve, while everyone clamours for their favourite piece of meat.

I do love roast chicken – a proper organic bird that has had freedom in its life. There's not that much of a secret to a good roast. First, get the best ingredients possible, either poultry or meat, and season generously. I like to put some crème fraîche or fromage frais into the cavity of a chicken, and perhaps add some thyme for flavour. I always begin roasting in a hot oven first, then I turn the oven down. And I baste. It's always better to cook big joints of meat on the bone and the most flavoursome meat is always closest to the bone. A leg of lamb has more flavour than a joint without a bone, and a rib roast of beef tastes better than a rolled joint. The meat even has a better texture, because it has been hung on the bone.

Always remember to take the bird or joint out of the fridge at least an hour before cooking. It needs to get up to room temperature before it goes into the oven, otherwise the centre of the meat is cold and the roast won't cook evenly.

Resting is vital. The longer you can rest the meat, the better. I serve a roast of venison that I rest for over an hour and it is absolutely perfectly pink inside. It isn't cold or overdone. It's just as it should be – completely tender with all the juices in the meat. For a leg of lamb or a rib of beef, you need to rest the meat for at least half an hour. Forty minutes is better. And you can happily rest it for an hour. Resting is not so important for white meat, but it is good to rest roast chicken and game for a while.

ROAST CHICKEN

There are many ways to roast a chicken, but the most important thing is, of course, to start off with a good-quality bird. I like to put a big tablespoon of yoghurt or crème fraîche in the cavity and then rub the skin with some oil, salt and pepper. Place the chicken on a roasting tray with a little oil and begin to roast in a preheated oven at 220°C/Gas 7 for 10 minutes. Then turn the oven down to 180°C/Gas 4 for about an hour for a 2kg bird.

As with all roasts, a few vegetables added to the roasting tray help to make a delicious jus as well as being a tasty accompaniment. I like to add 2 onions, 2 carrots, 2 or 3 stalks of celery and 2 fennel bulbs, trimmed, peeled and quartered, after about 10 minutes. You can also add bulbs of new season's garlic which you simply cut in half.

POMMES ANNA

Take a round cake tin measuring about 24cm wide by 6cm deep and grease liberally with butter.

Peel and slice 6–8 potatoes without washing them. Toss the sliced potatoes in a large bowl with a little clarified butter or oil, salt, pepper and some chopped thyme. Now carefully layer the slices of potato in the tin, taking care to arrange them in a spiral, flower-like fashion. Once the tin is full, cover with a buttered paper and place on the stove over medium heat for 5 or 6 minutes. Then bake in a hot oven at 200°C/Gas 6 for 30 minutes. Turn the oven down to 160°C/Gas 3 for a further 30 minutes.

Take the tin out of the oven. Place another tin of the same size on top and put a can or similar weight inside to press the Pommes Anna down. Leave to cool with the weight on top for 20 minutes, then turn it out and slice to serve.

ROAST LEG OF LAMB

New season's lamb is one of my favourite roasts. My preference is for a leg cooked on the bone, but if you're cooking shoulder it's best to pot roast or braise; it will always be better for it.

The traditional French method is to stud the leg of lamb with slivers of garlic. Make six incisions in the leg of lamb and insert a piece of garlic into each. Rub the leg with a little olive oil, salt and pepper. If you are not very partial to garlic, use some sprigs of rosemary and/or pitted, good-quality olives instead. Place the lamb on a hot roasting tray with a little more oil and sear over medium heat on top of the stove until golden on all sides. Place in a preheated oven at 200°C/Gas 6 for 10 minutes.

Then add some vegetables to the tray to roast with the lamb – garlic cloves, onions, carrots, celery and par-boiled potatoes. Add a generous amount of butter, put the roast back in the oven and turn down to 180°C/Gas 4 for 40 minutes for nicely pink lamb. Baste and turn the vegetables two or three times.

Remove the lamb from the oven and set aside in a warm place to rest. Take out the vegetables and keep them warm on a serving tray. Pour off the excess fat and place the roasting tray over high heat. Add a little water, bring to the boil and add a knob of fresh butter to the jus.

ROAST GUINEA FOWL WITH CHICKPEAS AND OLIVES

SERVES 4

120g chickpeas
1 bay leaf
1 sprig of rosemary
12 cloves garlic
1 oven-ready guinea fowl
1 tablespoon crème fraîche
4 tablespoons olive oil

1 tablespoon butter
24 olives, pitted
60ml Madeira
4 anchovies, chopped
1 small bunch basil,
   coarsely chopped
salt, pepper

Soak the chickpeas overnight in cold water, then rinse and drain. Cover with fresh water, add the bay leaf and rosemary and bring to the boil. Gently simmer for 45 minutes or until tender – you may have to top up with boiling water. Once the chickpeas are cooked, leave them to cool in the water. Peel the garlic cloves, put them in a saucepan and cover with cold water. Add a pinch of salt and bring to the boil. Drain and repeat this three times. This will make the garlic tender, sweet and less aggressive to taste. Set aside.

Season the guinea fowl and add the crème fraîche to the cavity, along with some seasoning. Put the bird in a roasting tray with the olive oil and sear on all sides over medium heat on the top of the stove. Place in a hot oven, 180°C/Gas 4, and add the butter. Roast for about 40 minutes, basting frequently. When the bird is done, remove from the roasting pan and set aside in a warm place to rest.

Place the roasting tray over a medium to high flame and add the olives, drained chickpeas (reserve a little of the water) and garlic. Cook, and stir a little for 4–5 minutes. Pour in the Madeira and 4 tablespoons of the cooking water from the chickpeas. Boil for 5 minutes, then add the anchovies, lots of pepper, the juices from the guinea fowl cavity and any more that have run. Just before serving, add the chopped basil and a drizzle of good olive oil.

ROAST PHEASANT
WITH ENDIVE CREAM

SERVES 2

1 oven-ready hen pheasant
2 tablespoons olive oil
2 tablespoons butter
2 shallots, peeled and sliced
2 large endives, sliced
2 teaspoons demerara sugar
30ml Madeira
150ml double cream
salt, pepper

Season the cavity of the pheasant with salt and pepper and place it in a heated, cast-iron casserole dish with the olive oil. Once the pheasant is seared on all sides, add the butter and continue to cook over medium heat until the butter is foaming. Put the bird on its side and then place in the preheated oven at 180°C/Gas 4 for 10 minutes. Turn the bird onto its other side for a further 10 minutes, and finally on its back for 10 minutes. Take the bird out and drain any juices from the cavity into the pan. Place the bird in a warm place, cover loosely and leave to rest.

Pour off the excess fat from the pan and return to the heat. Add the shallots, followed by the endives. Season well with salt, pepper and the sugar. Stir well and cook over moderate to high heat until the endives start to wilt. Now pour in the Madeira and, once this has boiled, add the cream and simmer for 10 minutes. Place the pheasant back in the pan with the endives and any juices that have run from the bird. Put the lid on and cook in the oven for a further 10 minutes. Bring to the table to carve. Best served with boiled potatoes.

I look back on my early childhood in Kent as an absolutely idyllic time. When he wasn't cooking for the Cazalets, my father was always around, digging in the garden, playing games with us and cooking. Although he must have been very busy, he did have time for me. We used to go fishing together a lot for pike, perch, carp and such like.

I didn't speak a word of English until I went to school, but I used to play very happily with Matthew, the boy who lived next door in the oast house. Heaven knows how we used to communicate, but we managed very well. We've never really lost touch since because when we moved to London, Matthew's family also moved to the city. We're still in contact, although he lives in New Zealand now.

I went to the village school and I found it difficult as first because I only spoke French. But the headmistress took me under her wing and looked after me. So I picked up English very quickly. It was a good school, with pretty green fields all around where we used to collect grass snakes.

My mother and father always asked me about the school food and they were curious about what English children ate. The food used to arrive in huge vats and be dished out to us. 'Meat and vegetables,' I would tell them every day, except Friday, when it was 'fish fingers and vegetables.' We had lots of stodgy puddings as well. I enjoyed them actually.

It was a huge shock when we moved to London so my father and uncle could open Le Gavroche. Suddenly he seemed to be gone from my life. He was still there, of course, but he wasn't around in the same way at all. He was always working, because Le Gavroche opened six nights a week. He was home on Sundays, but he was so exhausted he was often like a zombie.

We moved to Tooting Broadway, just off Garrett Lane, into a little semi-detached house, which gave onto a field belonging to a huge comprehensive school. Going to a new school was a shock too, moving from a small village school to an enormous orange-brick place. I didn't eat the meals there. I couldn't stomach them at all and very quickly decided to bring in my own packed lunches.

I didn't enjoy the school either, and only stayed there for two terms. Then I went to Highfield School, a smaller private school just off Trinity Road. It was better, but still not good, although I enjoyed it more there, particularly the sport. Strangely – or perhaps not so strangely – I never ate the school lunches there either.

My packed lunch was very, very different from everyone else's packed lunches. The other children had Marmite sandwiches, made with bleached white bread, and crisps. I had good rough bread with saucisson or Camembert, and always a piece of fruit. You could smell my lunch from one end of the classroom to the other. My mother used to pack it in a blue plastic tuckbox and there was always something tasty, always something from France.

Practically all our food was brought in from across the Channel. I remember my mother cooking sweetbreads when you couldn't buy them in this country. My friends were put off by a lot of the things we cooked, except for Matthew. He loved to come over and sample Mum's cooking, even if it was just something simple like an omelette and a properly dressed salad. Mum would send us to pick dandelion leaves on the common, and she mixed those into the salad to make it a bit more interesting, something I still do today. She also made gratin dauphinois which Matthew loved.

We spent all our time in each other's homes. His mother Jenny was a great cook too, but in an entirely different way. She was from New Zealand and made the most wonderful pavlovas. And her fruit crumble was to die for. Jenny also made something called toastie pies in a jaffle iron, with proper home-made bread, eggs and ham and lashings of butter. They were completely delicious.

I loved going to Matthew's house because it was so different, although, as in our house, food was a very important part of the daily routine, Matthew's parents were very relaxed and open and they did things like make their own muesli and yoghurt. Home was different, much more organised and orderly, so I liked the contrast.

We also spent a good deal of time at my uncle Michel's house. He had moved to Tooting, too, when Le Gavroche opened in London. Both my father and my uncle are extremely stubborn and have their

various ways of doing things in the kitchen. But their one ultimate goal is perfection and that's what binds them together. They will have furious arguments over how to cook an omelette, for example. Uncle likes them with a bit of colour. Father says no colour. But they're both delicious.

As in all Roux households, there were lots of gatherings round the table at Michel's house. I ate my first fondu there. I remember we had a cheese fondue at first, which I found a bit strong, and then the meat version, sizzling from the pot.

I was about nine or ten then, and about that time I had my first taste of caviar from a big tin. It must have been Christmas time, because I remember there were crackers around the table. My father had invited some friends to dinner and although my sister Danielle and I weren't allowed to be at the table for formal adult dinners, we did try a tiny bit of the caviar. The explosion of that wonderful salty taste in the mouth – I'll never forget it.

My grandparents, Jacqueline and Emile, with me and a doll from my grandmother's collection.

OMELETTE

Normally 2 eggs per person is enough for a snack, but if serving the omelette as a main meal allow 3–4. I use a cast-iron omelette pan, 20cm across.

Once the pan is hot, wipe it with a lightly oiled piece of cloth or absorbent paper. Break the eggs into a bowl and lightly season with salt and pepper. Put a generous knob of butter into the pan and turn up the heat. When the butter is foaming, pour in the eggs and cook for 20 seconds. Using the back of a fork, scrape the sides towards the middle and shake the pan while continuing to cook and stir. Once the eggs are cooked but still runny, stop stirring and take off the heat. Flip one half over towards the middle. Sprinkle over a mixture of chopped herbs (chives, parsley, chervil), and then roll the omelette over itself and onto a plate.

**Off on holiday
with the family.**

As well as raising our own pigeons and rabbits for the table, we also hunted for food. Snails and crayfish are two things that immediately come to mind. We used to go and collect snails in Kent, always after it had been raining, because once it rained, the snails came out. They had to be a special breed – the Burgundy snail, the French one you do with garlic butter. I'm sure the locals looked on with amusement and thought, 'Oh, my goodness, those French people are at it again.'

We continued to collect snails even after we moved to London. I remember waking early on a Sunday morning, being wrapped up in a blanket by my parents, getting into the car and going to Kent to collect snails. It took us a couple of hours to get there and we would come back with sackloads of snails, mainly for the restaurant.

Snails take a long time to prepare before you eat them. They have to be kept off food for several days so they purge themselves. Then you have to put some salt on them so they purge themselves a bit more. It's quite a laborious process.

We used to hunt for freshwater crayfish as well. This was in the days before the American crayfish invaded English waters. The English crayfish have a much lighter, green, shell as opposed to the American ones, which have an almost black shell. When I was a child, the English crayfish were in abundance in those beautiful streams in Kent.

We used to fish for them at night by flashlight and as soon as a car passed, my father told us we had to put our torches out very quickly so I think perhaps it wasn't quite legal. We kept hunting for crayfish after we moved to London from Kent because again, I remember being wrapped up in a blanket in the middle of the night and driving off with my parents.

My father had two methods of catching crayfish and both methods involved festering or rotten meat. He would gather

PREPARING SNAILS

Place the snails in a closed container pierced with holes. The holes must be small enough so as not to let the snails out but big enough for air to circulate. Put this in the garage or a cool sheltered place and leave the snails without food for 2–3 days. Then remove and put them in a bucket, liberally sprinkle with coarse sea salt, cover and leave for one day. Rinse well under cold water until the slime has all but gone and the snails are clean. Bring a court-bouillon(see p. 307) to the boil, add the snails and simmer for 1½ –2 hours, skimming off any scum from the surface. When the snails are tender, drain and discard the liquid. Then using a lobster pick or skewer, pull out the flesh from the shells. Remove the digestive track, which is found at the end of the snail, and discard. Rinse the shells and dry for further use. The snails can be used in any dish right away or stored in the fridge for 3 days.

up brambles and twigs and make a big fairly loose bundle. Then he'd put a piece of meat in the middle and toss it into the river. The idea was that the crayfish would be attracted by the meat and crawl into the bundle of twigs. We'd leave them for half an hour or so and then pull them in.

The other method we used was to make a little wire basket, a sort of keepnet, with a piece of rotting meat in the centre. Again, after about half an hour, we'd pull it up. You had to be very quick or you'd be nipped. That was one of my favourite games when I was little – to try to catch and land the crayfish without being nipped.

Once we were back home, we'd empty the fishing bags into our big, white, old-fashioned sink. Soon it would be teeming with crayfish darting all over the place. The crayfish were simply boiled, then dressed and eaten. The ones that went to the restaurant were prepared in much the same way.

Of course, no one can fish like that now. Many of the streams have dried up, and the native crayfish just don't exist in numbers like that today. I think they're more tender and sweet than the American crayfish, but the American ones still make very good eating. And the American crayfish are much more abundant because they are hardy, sturdy and reproduce very quickly.

We were, and still are, a typically French family, and very proud of our French food. But we were curious about English food as well, even though we didn't eat much of it. I was always fascinated by the English habit of tea. I had my first taste of this real Englishness soon after we moved to London.

My parents had a friend in Kent who I used to call Uncle Jim – his name was Jim Garrett and he had a paper-recycling business. We used to have the most wonderful fun playing in these huge piles of paper. Then we would have a proper old-fashioned English tea with fairy cakes, sponge cakes and sandwiches. It was never dinner, always tea because they were a very English family. I was so struck by that and how different their food was to ours.

Jim had a son called Lesley and we always kept in contact with Lesley over the years. He was a jack of all trades and did a lot of work for us. I still keep in contact with some of Lesley's children. We used to go fishing with Lesley, too, in St Mary's Bay in Kent. By then we were living in London, so we'd get up early and drive down and get into a speedboat we used when we went fishing. Lesley was very scatterbrained. With Lesley there was always something happening and it was always an adventure. There'd be my father, myself, Lesley and Lesley's son Tim in the boat, with only one lifejacket. It's a miracle we survived. Once we ran out of petrol about five miles from shore. Somehow we got back that time.

Once the lifeguards had to come out to rescue us. Another time we hit a sandbank, and the pin holding the propeller sheared off. Of course, Lesley didn't have a replacement. But we had such fun and the fishing was good in those days. We'd catch lots of different types of fish – sole, cod, plaice, flounder, and conger eel if we were lucky enough to fish near a wreck. It was always good fishing.

I've inherited my father's energy. He has amazing energy and so do I. So does my mother. Both of them could live on almost no sleep.

OLD-FASHIONED JAM

For each kilo of fruit, you need 800–900g caster sugar, depending on the natural sweetness of the fruit. If you're using strawberries or apricots cut them in half. Leave raspberries whole. Place the fruit in a stainless steel or glass bowl and add the sugar. Gently toss to coat the fruit, cover and chill for at least 24 hours.

Drain the fruit in a colander to collect the natural syrup. Cook this syrup to 108°C using a sugar thermometer. Then add the fruit and continue to simmer gently, stirring and skimming, for 15–20 minutes. Pour into clean, sealable jars. As this jam is not very sweet it is best kept cool and refrigerated once opened.

ORANGE MARMALADE

Wash the Seville oranges and place them in a big pot with cold water. Cover and bring to a gentle boil. Cook until the oranges are tender and easily pierced with a needle or fork – about 45 minutes. Drain and rinse under cold water.

Weigh the oranges and for every kilo, you will need a kilo of caster sugar. Put the sugar into a heavy pan, add just enough water to moisten and bring to the boil. Cut the oranges into quarters and remove the pips. Slice the quarters thinly, add them to the syrup and continue to simmer, skimming off any scum. After an hour, test by putting a spoonful of jam onto a plate to see if it sets. Pour into clean, sealable jars.

He was in the restaurant until late every night, and after it closed there was often a card game with the staff until the early hours.

From about the age of 13, my father would ask me to go to the markets with him during school holidays. He did this at least once a week. He'd wake me up at 1 or 2 in the morning, having only just closed the restaurant and come home. I'd get out of bed and off we'd go in our car or in the company van to the old Billingsgate fish market. The noise! Everyone was shouting and rushing over the old cobbled yard. I would duck to avoid the porters carrying huge loads on their heads, with their special flat caps. There was so much to see and to look out for, and everywhere was that wonderful smell of the sea and fresh fish.

I would just hang onto my father's coat tails as he rushed around the place. He paid for everything in cash, so there was money flying everywhere. It was my job to hang onto the satchel with the cash in it. We didn't use cheques. I remember my father arguing about the price of sole and other fish, bargaining hard before he agreed on the final deal.

We'd load the fish into the van and drive off to the meat market at Smithfield – yet another world of new smells and things to see.

Me with the catch of the day on one of our family fishing holidays.

My father would heave huge hindquarters of beef onto his shoulder and the porters got furious with him because no one except them was allowed to carry meat. That didn't stop Dad. He did it anyway. There was a lot of banter and a lot of jokes about the Frenchie. They'd call him Sacha after Sacha Distel or start singing Charles Aznavour songs as he walked around the market.

Then we'd drive down to Covent Garden, the old Covent Garden right in the middle of London, for the fruit and vegetables. My father would inspect everything very closely and always drive a hard bargain before buying. By then the van would be full and we'd deliver the food to the restaurants – we had two restaurants then, Le Gavroche and Le Poulbot.

There was always a lot of hard work in our family. That's the way our family is. We just do it and never look at the clock. But there are a lot of laughs as well, and we're always around food. Everything centres on food and we always consider everything related to food as being utterly serious.

Take the way my mother cooks an omelette. She would never do it any other way than this. For a start, she uses a proper cast-iron pan, not a Teflon pan. A good omelette doesn't need anything added – except possibly a drop of milk, although we never did that. She cooks her omelette very quickly with a lot of butter. A good omelette is cooked but runny in the middle and that is the secret of it. It should have a very slight colour to it and be folded – it must be folded to be a French omelette. Invariably we'll just put herbs in it, just snipped from the garden, or maybe some cheese. But it's not slapdash. Nothing is ever slapdash or in a hurry. To us, fast food is an omelette, a boiled egg or something like that.

You find that everywhere in France – there is always a structure to a meal, even in a staff canteen. There is a starter, a middle and an end. The food has to be put on the plate in a certain way. It's a reverence for food. Even if it's just a stew there has to be something to it. It isn't just tossed on the plate to be eaten any old way.

This is true through every level of French society, whether you're a taxi driver or a multi-millionaire. Even breakfast in France has a structure. There will be orange juice, your coffee, your bread, your butter. Even when having a snack, you'll sit down at the table. You lay the table, even if it's just for yourself. There is a knife and fork. You don't eat standing up, or over the sink or watching television. We have too much respect for our food ever to do that. In France, you're fiercely proud of your specialities and your suppliers – your local sausage, your butcher, your cheesemaker.

If you've only got ten minutes, you take those ten minutes to sit down and enjoy what you're eating. We don't see food as mere fuel. It goes back to the structure of the meal. You can't have a French meal without cheese, whether you have a starter or not. Sometimes the starter is just a few leaves of green salad, then your main course is of protein and a vegetable, then something sweet, even if it's as small as a little piece of chocolate or a piece of fruit. It means you enjoy what you eat, which is so much better for you and makes you appreciative of what you've got.

All my family are like that. Perhaps it's just as well, because we're a big family and we're close because we all share the same passion for food. There is my aunt Martine who used to look after me and my sister a lot when we were children, and of course my uncle Michel, his first wife Françoise and their children – Christine, Francine and Alain, who now runs the Waterside Inn.

My other aunt, Liliane is married to a wonderful charcutier, Paul. For a couple of years, my father and Paul ran a charcuterie, Le Cochon Rose, next to Le Gavroche in Lower Sloane Street. But I think it was a bit ahead of its time and it closed after a few years.

My mother's family is passionate about food, too. My uncle Jean would travel across Paris to get the best cheese or meat for a special family meal. Jean was a darling of a man. He loved his food and wine, but in a way that meant he always sought perfection. Jean and his wife Danielle were not particularly well off, so delicacies had to be saved up for. Then he would spend all day searching Paris to get the very best ingredients from the very best shops to make the meal special, not particularly by cooking because they weren't chefs, but special because it was the best chicken, the best gâteau,

The family tree

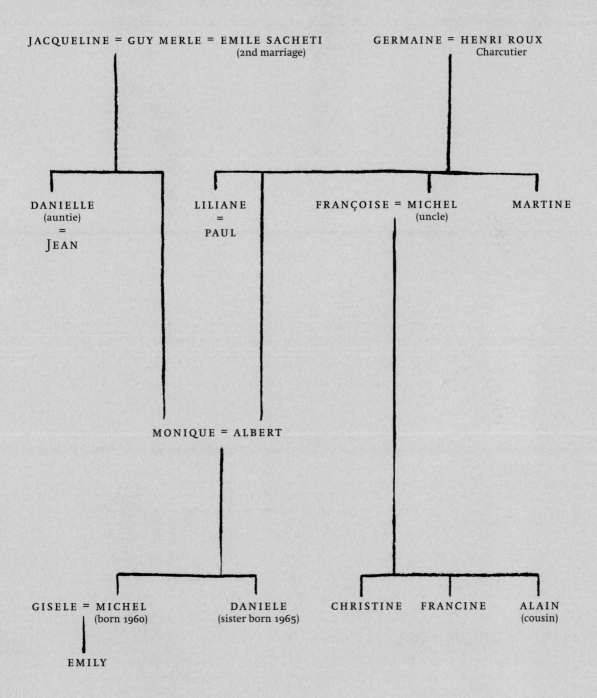

JACQUELINE = GUY MERLE = EMILE SACHETI
(2nd marriage)

GERMAINE = HENRI ROUX
Charcutier

DANIELLE
(auntie)
=
Jean

LILIANE
=
PAUL

FRANÇOISE = MICHEL
(uncle)

MARTINE

MONIQUE = ALBERT

GISELE = MICHEL
(born 1960)

DANIELE
(sister born 1965)

CHRISTINE   FRANCINE   ALAIN
(cousin)

EMILY

TOP: A family party at
the Roux household in
the late 1950s.
BELOW: Three generations
– me with my father and
my daughter Emily.

the best cheese. Family occasions were always a celebration and Jean would go to the best butcher for a fillet for my father to roast. Again, he might have to go to the other side of Paris and he would come home hours and hours later. Sometimes it might be just a little box of chocolates, but it would have cost him a fortune and it would be our special treat.

It was the same with wine. Jean was probably the best host you could ever ask for. Everything had to be perfect. He is sorely missed. Even though he didn't work with food – he worked in insurance – he loved it just as much as the rest of the family.

So it's not surprising that I chose to go into the family business. I genuinely don't think I could have done anything else. There was no other option. The only choice was when to leave school and for me, the sooner I got out of school and began my career the better. I liked Emanuel, the last school I went to, and I had good friends there. But I wanted to get out and start work.

LETTUCE SOUP

My grandmother Germaine used to make this classic French soup.
The original recipe calls for new season, tender round lettuce.
However, being a good housekeeper with monetary constraints,
she used any kind of lettuce, and only the outer dark-green leaves
that were not as palatable as the sweet hearts in a salad.

SERVES 4

100g dark outer leaves of lettuce, washed
1 tablespoon butter
300g potatoes, peeled and diced
200g ripe tomatoes, quartered
1.4 litres boiling water
salt
crème fraîche

Tear the lettuce leaves into pieces if large, then
sweat in the butter. Add the diced potato and
quartered tomatoes. Continue to cook for a
further 5 minutes, then add the water. Simmer
for 20 minutes or until the potatoes are cooked.

Season to taste, then blend until smooth or pass
though a fine sieve if preferred. Delicious hot or
cold with or without a good spoonful of crème
fraîche. Add a garnish of lettuce heart and a little
chopped tomato if you like.

HAM AND CAULIFLOWER TERRINE

Wonderful for a picnic and even better with the addition of a few shavings of summer truffle.

8 slices Parma ham
300g cauliflower, cut into florets
1 tablespoon butter
200g cooked ham, cut into medium-sized dice
4 eggs
200ml double cream
salt, pepper, nutmeg

Take a terrine or cake tin measuring about 28 x 8cm and double line with clingfilm. Then line the tin with slices of Parma ham, making sure they overlap.

Boil the cauliflower florets in salted water until tender, then drain and leave to cool. Heat the butter in a frying pan and toss in the diced ham. Once the ham is lightly browned, drain and add to the cauliflower. Beat the eggs with the cream and season with salt, pepper and nutmeg. Add the ham and cauliflower to the terrine, then pour in the egg and cream mixture.

Fold over the overlapping ham and clingfilm, then place the terrine in a pan of simmering water and bake for 1 hour at 140°C/Gas 1. Leave to cool completely before taking the terrine out of the tin. If you do have a truffle, add some shavings just before serving.

LEEK SALAD EGG VINAIGRETTE

When leeks are young and tender there can be no better way
to enjoy them than in this simple French classic.

SERVES 4

16 leeks, washed
2 tablespoons Dijon mustard
2 tablespoons red wine vinegar
salt and pepper
4–6 tablespoons water
300ml vegetable or peanut oil
2 eggs, hard-boiled
1 bunch chives, snipped

Trim the dark green tops of the leeks, leaving about 3cm of the
light green. Cook the leeks in boiling salted water until tender
(about 6 minutes). Drain and lay flat on a rack to cool while you
make the vinaigrette.

Place the mustard, red wine vinegar and seasoning in a bowl
with a little of the water. Whisk as if making a mayonnaise,
slowly adding the oil to emulsify the vinaigrette. Add a little
more water if the mixture becomes too thick.

Cut the leeks in half lengthways and place on a dish or plate.
Scatter over the chopped egg and snipped chives. Drizzle with
the vinaigrette and eat before the leeks get cold.

VEAL KIDNEYS WITH THREE-MUSTARD SAUCE

A classic, and probably the most popular offal dish to be served at Le Gavroche over the years. Best served with tagliatelle and spinach.

SERVES 4

2 veal kidneys
1 tablespoon oil
salt and pepper
½ tablespoon butter
2 shallots
50ml white wine
50ml chicken stock (see p. 304)
200ml double cream

THREE-MUSTARD MIX

2 teaspoons Dijon mustard
2 teaspoons tarragon mustard
4 teaspoons coarse grain mustard

Remove the fat and any sinew from the kidneys and cut into bite-sized pieces. Heat up a thick-based sauté pan or a cast-iron skillet and add a little oil or, better still, some rendered kidney fat. Sear the kidneys and season with a little salt and pepper. Remove after a couple of minutes and put the kidneys to drain in a colander – they should be very pink.

In the same pan, add a small knob of butter and a good tablespoon of finely chopped shallots. Do not let them colour. Pour in a splash of dry white wine and when this has almost boiled away, add a little chicken stock and double cream to make the sauce. Simmer for 4–5 minutes but do not let it reduce too much. Add the kidneys and enough mustard mix to give the sauce body. Do not let the sauce boil as it will become bitter. Serve immediately.

AVOCADO AND BACON SALAD WITH CHILLI

SERVES 4

4 ripe avocados
juice of 1 lemon
1 tablespoon chopped flat-leaf parsley
2 spring onions
1 medium red chilli
8 slices of smoked, dry-cured bacon
1 tablespoon red wine vinegar
4 tablespoons olive oil
salt, pepper

Cut the avocados in half and remove the stones and peel. Cut the flesh into long, chunky strips and toss in the lemon juice to keep the avocado from discolouring. Pick and wash the parsley, then roughly chop. Wash and thinly slice the spring onions and set aside with the parsley. Thinly slice the chilli, with or without the seeds to taste.

Cut the bacon into strips and place in a non-stick pan with a drop of olive oil. Cook until golden but not dry, then take off the heat.

Place the avocado, parsley, spring onions and chilli in a large salad bowl and season lightly with salt and pepper. Add the bacon, vinegar and remaining olive oil. Toss and serve immediately.

TARTE FLAMBÉE

SERVES 4

300g onions, peeled and thinly sliced
4 tablespoons vegetable oil
250g smoked streaky bacon
150g fromage frais
4 tablespoons crème fraîche
salt, pepper
DOUGH
20g fresh yeast
220ml tepid water
350g bread flour
1 tablespoon olive oil
1 pinch of salt

First make the dough. Dissolve the yeast in the tepid water and add the flour, oil and salt. Knead well into an elastic smooth dough, working it for at least 10 minutes. This can be done in a food mixer with the dough-hook attachment. Once the dough is made, cover and leave to double in volume. Knock back and on a floured surface roll out to a rectangle. This should measure about 40 x 22cm and be as thin as possible. Place the dough on a non-stick baking tray. Moisten the edges with a pastry brush and turn over the edges to form a rim 1cm wide. Place in the refrigerator to rest.

Preheat the oven to 230°C/Gas 8. Put the onions in a wide saucepan with 2 tablespoons of the oil and cook over a medium heat. They should be tender in 5 or 6 minutes. Season with salt and pepper and leave to cool. Cut the bacon into small batons and sprinkle over the dough, followed by the onions. Mix the fromage frais with the crème fraîche and spread this evenly over the bacon and onions. Drizzle over the remaining oil and add a little more pepper. Cook for 10 minutes, or until well coloured and cooked, and then devour immediately.

ELDERFLOWER BEIGNETS

Late spring is the time to pick fragrant elderflowers. They can be made into a deliciously heady cordial to mix with champagne or to enhance a fruit salad. But if you really want to wow and impress, try dipping the flowers in batter and frying. Then just dust with icing sugar and enjoy.

SERVES 4

50g cornflour
200g plain flour
½ teaspoon bicarbonate of soda
500ml carbonated water
light vegetable oil
12 elderflower heads
icing sugar

Put the cornflour, flour and bicarbonate into a bowl and mix with a fork. Slowly add the water. The mix should be fairly wet and grainy; do not overwork.

Heat the vegetable oil in a large pan. Dip the flowers in the batter, gently shaking off the excess, then drop into hot oil until crisp and golden. Dust with icing sugar.

OREILLETTES

These fritters are served as a sweet treat or with coffee after dinner. They come from the Ardèche region in France and my mother-in-law, Raymonde, makes very good ones. In Lyon, they are called bugnes and differ slightly in thickness and sometimes in flavour. You can add vanilla, orange-flower water or any number of flavourings.

MAKES ABOUT 40

200g plain flour
80g caster sugar
2 tablespoons melted butter or vegetable oil
2 eggs
½ tablespoon orange-flower water
1 pinch salt
vegetable oil

Sift the flour into a bowl, add the other ingredients (except the oil) and mix well. Continue to knead the dough until it is smooth and elastic, adding a little water if necessary. Cover and chill for an hour.

On a floured surface (wood is best), roll the dough out to a thickness of 2mm. You can stretch the paste with your fingertips, but be careful not to make any holes. Using a fluted pastry cutter or knife, cut the paste into odd shapes measuring about 4 x 8 cm.

Heat the oil in a large pan or deep-fryer and drop in the shapes a few at a time. As they puff and rise, turn them over to brown on both sides. Once they are crisp and golden, remove and drain them on a kitchen towel. Dust with icing sugar and devour.

MARINATED STRAWBERRIES AND CHANTILLY CREAM

30–50g caster sugar
500g strawberries, hulled
1 vanilla pod
200ml whipping cream
60ml Cointreau
30g icing sugar
2 teaspoons vanilla essence
2 tablespoons crème fraîche

Sprinkle caster sugar over the hulled strawberries according to the sweetness of the fruit and your taste. Split the vanilla pod, scrape out the seeds and place them in a clean, cold bowl with the whipping cream. Add the scraped pod to the strawberries along with the Cointreau and gently toss them around. Cover the strawberries with clingfilm and refrigerate for at least one hour but no more than two.

Whisk the whipping cream until it comes together. Add the icing sugar, vanilla essence and crème fraîche and continue to whisk until firm. Chill until needed.

I serve this dessert in individual glass bowls or glasses. Place some strawberries and marinade in each glass, followed by a generous spoon of cream. You could also use a piping bag with a star nozzle to add the cream if you prefer. If you have time, some strawberries dipped in caramel finish the dish off a treat.

OLD-FASHIONED SHORTBREAD

These classics are so easy to make and keep well in an airtight box – but once cooked why keep them?

MAKES ABOUT 20 DEPENDING ON SIZE
230g plain flour
75g caster sugar
160g butter, room temperature
1 teaspoon vanilla extract
granulated sugar for dusting

Mix the flour and sugar together. Using your fingertips, gently work in the soft butter and vanilla extract. The paste should just come together – do not overwork. Wrap in clingfilm and chill for an hour.

Preheat the oven to 180°C/Gas 4. Roll the paste out to 1cm thick and cut into rounds or fingers. Prick with a fork and bake for about 25 minutes until cooked, but don't let them colour too much. Leave the shortbread to cool in the tin for a short while before putting them on a rack. Dust with some granulated sugar before they are completely cool.

PEARS IN RED WINE

SERVES 6

6 pears, still a little firm
1 bottle red wine (Pinot or Gamay)
200g caster sugar
1 cinnamon stick
1 vanilla pod, split
6 black peppercorns
1 strip of orange peel
4 tablespoons crème de cassis

Peel and core the pears, taking care to leave the stalks in place. Put all the remaining ingredients, except the crème de cassis, into a pan and bring to the boil. Add the pears, make sure they are submerged and cover with greaseproof paper. Simmer for 20 minutes or until tender, then leave to cool. Add the crème de cassis and refrigerate overnight.

If you want a thicker syrup, decant the liquid and boil until it is reduced by one-third. Serve with crème fraîche. If you like, decorate the pears with thin strips of orange peel cooked in sugar syrup.

Being a Roux

When I was growing up I wasn't really aware that my father and my uncle were so famous and that the name of Roux had become synonymous with everything to do with the finest of French food in England. It was only when I left school and began working that I realised my surname was both a help and a hindrance. There was, and still is, enormous pressure to succeed and to compete. When I was working in France as an apprentice, fellow chefs would say, 'He's the son of the famous Roux brothers'. I was proud of course, but there was so much to live up to because my father and uncle were seen as the pioneers of gastronomy and the first ones to plant the French flag in England.

My father helped me a huge amount in guiding my career moves and exposing me on a daily basis to the best possible food and wine. My mother did, too. From both of them, I learned a great respect for food and that if you wanted to eat well, you had to search out the best ingredients, even if that proved difficult.

And in the early days, it was incredibly difficult. It was almost impossible to find good ingredients in England. But in the Roux family, you don't just shrug your shoulders and say it doesn't matter and you'll find something else. You go out and find what you need. In this, my parents were a true inspiration to me.

When Le Gavroche opened in April 1967, in its original premises in Lower Sloane Street, Britain was still not in the Common Market and no one was allowed to import food except for their own consumption. Even then, reams of paperwork were sometimes required. It seems hard to believe now, but at that time most people regarded olive oil as medicine for unplugging blocked ears. For frying, everyone used lard, dripping or a poorer-quality vegetable oil, which was very coarse and heavy. They also used butter, of course, but even the butter wasn't good at that time

OPPOSITE: Michel and Albert Roux at Le Gavroche in Lower Sloane Street, 1967.

in England – it was very oversalted. The best butter you could get then came from New Zealand or Denmark.

It was a pretty dire culinary situation for people like my father and uncle, who were obsessed with producing the finest French food, but that didn't deter them at all. While my father and Michel worked 18- to 20-hour days in the restaurant, my mother went off to Paris to find all the wonderful ingredients needed to make dinner or lunch at Le Gavroche as perfect as it could possibly be. All the things we take for granted now – cornfed chickens, ducklings, hams, spices, even sel de Guérande – were nowhere to be found in shops in England. We had to bring in our own butter for the table – Beurre d'Isigny – and you simply couldn't find things like proper sea salt anywhere in the country. There was no Brie, no Camembert, no Roquefort, nothing.

So at least once a week, more often twice, my mother would get into her big old Peugeot estate car and set off from Tooting for Paris. She'd leave very early in the morning, drive to the coast, take the ferry to France and then drive into the capital. She'd buy what she needed, load up the car and stay with my aunt and uncle overnight. Then she'd drive back to London first thing in the morning. And she'd do it on her own, because my father would be working in the restaurant. As kids, my sister and I accepted that as completely normal, something that had to be done. Someone would come in to baby-sit us while she was away. Often, a relative or a family friend would be staying in the house anyway, so there was always someone to look after us while she went on shopping trips.

Everything, not just the obvious delicacies like foie gras or poulet de Bresse, had to come from Paris. That was my mother's job. There was a speciality shop on the rue de Belles Feuilles which sold the best poulet de Bresse in the city as well as other fine ingredients.

My mother used this shop, what we call an 'épicerie fine', as a kind of depot while she rushed all over Paris to buy things, and then she'd head for home. The car would be fully loaded, just packed full of food. Then came the difficult part. She had to get

The Roux family on the way back from France. Those cases were packed full of food!

all the supplies back to England without being stopped at customs because, strictly speaking, what she was doing was illegal.

Occasionally she'd be stopped by the customs officers. It must have looked a bit suspicious – a woman on her own in a car full of food, even if it was camouflaged with blankets or clothes and other things. The customs men would open up the boxes and my mother would try to fend them off with a bit of charm. But sometimes it didn't work. She'd try saying that the food was for personal consumption, but if you've got 50 chickens as well as foie gras and sausages and God knows what else, it's hard to convince anybody that all this food is just for one family.

Under the law then, customs could confiscate the lot until you could provide a valid veterinary certificate, as well as a lot of other documentation. Of course, if it wasn't forthcoming within three days, everything would be destroyed. And on occasion it was because we couldn't get the certificates in time. So more often than not, if my mother was stopped, we lost the lot.

That happened sometimes, but not too often. My mother would use different ports all the time to try and not look too suspicious, and take different boats at different times. There were plenty of options – Dover, Folkestone, Southampton – and because she travelled at different times she didn't get the same officers on duty. Sometimes she used Lydd airport, because up until the mid 1970s you could put the car in a plane from Lydd Airport in Kent and fly over to Le Touquet, then drive from Le Touquet to Paris.

Occasionally during school holidays, my sister Danielle and I would go with her to make the trip look like a family outing. When we went with her, not only was the boot filled with food, but we also had huge, old-fashioned trunks strapped onto the roof of the car and they were crammed full of food too. Once the customs stopped the car when I was in it. It was terrifying. They confiscated everything and incinerated it. There was nothing we could do about it except go home, rest up, then get back in the car and set off for Paris again through another port.

It wasn't just a one-way street, though. When wild salmon, sea trout and game were in season in England, my mother would take these to France, to restaurants in Paris. Occasionally she would get stopped on the way into Paris by the French customs, but it was a lot easier on the other side. Of course, there was no way that the French customs would have destroyed that food, no way at all.

My mother did that for at least a decade after Le Gavroche opened. She was a good driver, but not a slow one. We used to call her Fangio, after the racing driver, and she delighted in breaking her own time records getting to and from Paris. She just drove and drove until the car finally gave out. I remember the Peugeot literally collapsed one day on the périphérique, the ring road around Paris. Not only did the engine blow up, but it also fell out onto the road!

Nothing mattered to either of my parents except getting hold of the best ingredients, the best food. They would go to any lengths to obtain what they wanted and they didn't trust anyone else to choose the food. Later, of course, the suppliers came to them, but in the early days they did everything themselves. It was all part of their dedication to their work and I learned from that. Even now, I still check all the produce for Le Gavroche myself.

I was never afraid of hard work. I'd seen so much of it in my family and I knew from them that if you loved what you did, then it was fun and you never resented the time or effort it took. My father helped me a huge amount, but he didn't believe in just giving his children things, even when life got much easier with the success of Le Gavroche. Oh no, we weren't just handed things on a plate. We had to earn them. I worked every school holidays in restaurants doing all the menial tasks. When I was 13, I went to work in the kitchen of Le Poulbot restaurant, doing basic kitchen prep. I used to get there at 7 in the morning, peel potatoes and cut the chips. Everything was done by hand, including the washing up. The kitchen had to be completely spotless and everything had to be scrubbed clean. Every pot had to be polished so you could see your face in it. It was tough, but it was a good lesson, and I try to be the same way with our daughter Emily. Everything has a value and you need to realise that from an early age.

CHIPS COOKED IN GOOSE FAT

You need good-quality potatoes such as Rooster. Peel the potatoes, cut them into chips and leave to soak in cold water for at least an hour. Then drain and place in a pan of cold, salted water. Bring to the boil and simmer for 2–3 minutes. Drain in a colander and then on a clean tea towel. The potatoes should be still firm but almost cooked.

Heat the goose fat in a heavy frying pan – test with a piece of bread to see if it sizzles and fries. Shallow-fry the chips until golden and cooked, then drain and sprinkle with a good coarse sea salt, such as a sel de Guérande or Maldon, before serving.

My daughter Emily,
aged 13 and already
a keen cook.

I used the money I earned to buy teenage luxuries. A stereo system
was one of the first things I bought and I treasured it. I also bought
my own racing bike, a ten-speed, orange Holdsworth. It was my
pride and joy and once I rode it to Brighton and back. It was the
same for my sister. She always had jobs or schemes to make herself
some pocket money. Once on a family holiday, I picked some
mushrooms and my sister, being a good businesswoman, soon had
them in a box out on the road with a For Sale sign. She was only 11.

While we were, and still are, a hard-working family, we also knew
how to have a good time. I used to go fishing with my grandfather
Emile. He was my maternal grandfather, the second husband of my
grandmother. Emile was a hairdresser, one of the best in Paris so
he said, and he was also a very keen fisherman. During the long
school holidays in summer, my parents would rent a little cottage,
somewhere in the south of France or Brittany, and drive my sister
and me down there to stay with Emile for two or three weeks.
We did this from when I was eight to when I was about 12. I had
a wonderful time with Emile, because he was so patient. He was
a big man, with huge hands, or so they seemed to me because
I was so small then. He was always immaculately dressed and

smoked like a trooper. He had great yellow stains on his hands and, of course, it was smoking that got him in the end.

He was absolutely meticulous in the preparation of his fishing tackle and I think I may have learned that quality from him – how not to skimp on preparation time and to make sure things are done properly. Every night before we went fishing, he would spend at least an hour preparing everything and making sure it was all clean and in good order. That way we would not waste time or be fiddling around in the dark on the river bank in the morning. Then he would prepare a Thermos flask of his own special bait mixture. This had the most wonderful smell of corn and star anise. I can smell it now – it was good enough to eat.

My grandfather swore by this as bait and the fish came – carp, roach and tench, a big slimy fish, a bottom feeder. We caught the odd pike, but most of the time we caught little fish like whitebait. Emile would just fry them simply. They were so delicious.

GRANDFATHER EMILE'S BAIT RECIPE

Pour boiling water over dried corn in a Thermos flask, then add three or four star anise or a dash of Pernod. Close the flask and leave the mixture to stand overnight before using. Perfect for carp, roach, dace and barbel.

After our holiday with Emile, Mum and Dad would pick us up and we'd go on to somewhere else in France. Again, we went fishing together a lot. One place I particularly remember was in the Dordogne and we used to catch hundreds of little fish – perch, gudgeon, bleak and roach – and take them back to the house. I used to help gut the fish, then roll them in flour and deep fry them. We had the most wonderful meals of deep-fried fish. They were scrumptious, absolutely beautiful.

We went to Spain on other holidays. My father would just pack us into the car – we always had clapped-out cars – and we'd drive down to Spain in one day's continuous driving to Meha in Galicia. A good client of Le Gavroche had a house there and he and my father had become friends. One year in Meha, when I was 11 or 12, I had my first taste of honeycomb. The family kept bees and the beekeeper would bring us great slabs of honey. There were still bees coming out of it. I'd never seen honeycomb before and it seemed amazing that you could eat the lot. That first bite into the honeycomb was wonderful – the waxy taste of the comb and the honey dripping down my chin. I loved it and all the other smells of the flowers and the heat. They were very happy times.

I remember one year the car exploded on the way and it had to be fixed, which took a week or so. We didn't mind at all because there was a lake near the village and my father blagged his way into getting us some fishing rods. He got some meat and left it on the windowsill to rot. After two days, we had maggots galore and off we went fishing again.

Even after I left school and started my apprenticeship in Paris, we spent family holidays together. They were simple, but completely wonderful. We spent summer holidays in Ireland in a tiny village called Cahersiveen, just off Valentia Island, west of Cork. All of us – my parents, my sister and I and our black Labrador, Gavroche – went there for almost a full month several years running. Sometimes friends would come with us as well. We went deep-sea fishing every day, and every night we'd cook what we'd caught. It was usually just tossed in flour and fried – and it always tasted delicious.

Once we caught some skate and we brought it back and cooked it that evening. It tasted terrible, like rubber. We couldn't eat it under any circumstances. The next day, my father mentioned this to one of the local fishermen and he laughed his socks off. In a thick Irish accent, he explained to my father that you shouldn't eat any sort of ray on the day you catch it. You had to leave it in the refrigerator for a day or so to let it soften. Most flatfish – turbot, sole or brill – are better the following day. Even my father, the great chef, didn't know that.

I remember my mother catching a skate off the Skellig Rocks. It was massive thing weighing 136 pounds and actually an Irish specimen. I caught 32-pound dogfish and my father caught a 52-pound conger eel. Some days when the sea was too rough to go out on the boat we'd walk for hours and then fish off the rocks. Looking back now, it was incredibly dangerous really, with huge waves crashing at our feet, but that never occurred to us. If the weather was very bad we'd fish off the pier and Gavroche would jump in and go swimming. She just loved the water.

Sometimes we'd go to the local pub after dinner for Irish coffee and play pool. My father is not a good pool player, but somehow I seem to remember he won a fair bit of the time. They were wonderful holidays, just wonderful.

Cooking fresh fish

I had the freshest fish I've ever eaten on a fishing trip in Ireland, when I was 15 or 16. We were jigging for mackerel – by that I mean using a special kind of line with several hooks that you jerk up and down to attract the fish. On this boat, the skipper had a tradition of immediately cooking and eating the first mackerel that were caught. So when five or six fish came up, he whipped off the fillets, and rinsed them in a bucket of seawater. He had a non-stick pan on a gas ring, with no oil or butter, and he just chucked them in. I swear the fillets were still moving in the pan! No salt or pepper... the fish didn't need it. The smell and the taste were absolutely unbelievable. We had a bit of soda bread as well and we washed the lot down with a flask of tea. That was the best, freshest piece of mackerel I've ever tasted.

Oily fish, like herrings, mackerel and sardines, do need to be eaten quickly after catching. The fresher they are the better they taste. They spoil faster than white fish, like cod and bass. The recent trend for eating fish such as gurnard, pollock and coley is good because they are sustainable species. That is great and should be commended. At Le Gavroche we've been serving gurnard, mackerel and pollock for 20 years. It's not new for us. But others may now be jumping on the bandwagon and selling these cheaper fish at the same old expensive prices.

Gurnard is a wonderful fish, but I do love turbot. It has to be the king of all fish. It's flavoursome and meaty. But gone are the days when you could pick up a 10kg turbot. It is over fished and very rare now. And it commands a huge price. If I get a turbot in the kitchen, it's not unusual for it to cost £300.00. And there is a fair bit of waste on a turbot. So once I've trimmed it down, a portion of turbot can cost me £15.00 before I've even done anything to it.

Generally speaking, it's best to cook fish simply. We serve turbot grilled on the bone with a very simple sauce, a beurre blanc and chives, and a vegetable garnish. It doesn't need anything else. A hollandaise is a wonderful accompaniment for fish. It's got a bit of acidity and it's smooth and velvety. Oily fish like mackerel can handle spices better than white fish, and aggressive grilling is good for bringing out their flavour. But as a general rule, you should be very respectful when cooking fish. The Chinese way of cooking sea bass or grouper – steaming it whole and then pouring over a dressing, almost a vinaigrette, of spring onions, fermented black beans and oil, often with some citrus juice and light soy sauce – is very flavoursome, but it doesn't mask the taste of the fish because steaming does retain flavour. The Caribbean and Indian style of rubbing spices into fish is a bit too aggressive for my taste, but others love this. Fish and chips? I love fish and chips. Gurnard is very good for putting in batter and frying.

The sea is just a huge larder. There is so much in there. There has been great progress in farming fish too, which I'm for in many ways. It's good that we can offer salmon in the shops at an affordable price and most of it is reasonable quality. I tend not to use farmed fish at Le Gavroche, however, because although it is good, it's not as good as wild.

GRILLED MACKEREL WITH MUSTARD

Gut the mackerel, cut off the head and fins and rinse under cold water. Make 5 incisions across the fish equally on each side.

Liberally smear Dijon mustard over the fish and into the holes made by the cuts. Place the mackerel under a hot grill for 10 minutes or until golden, then turn over and cook for a further 6–8 minutes. This is the simplest and best way to enjoy mackerel.

FRIED POLLACK

In my view, pollack is as good as cod when it's fresh and cooked properly. When on holiday in Ireland we never tired of eating this beautiful, flaky, firm-textured fish.

SERVES 4

pollack fillets
seasoned flour
oil
butter
1 lemon

Cut the fillets into portions of about 160g each, with the skin on. Dust in seasoned flour and place in a hot frying pan with a little smoking vegetable oil. Turn down the heat and continue to cook until golden on both sides, then add a generous spoonful of butter to finish cooking the fish.

Once the butter has turned to a nutty brown colour, take the pan off the heat and remove the cooked fish. Add a good squeeze of lemon to the juices in the pan, stir and spoon over the fish.

POACHED LING HOLLANDAISE

Ling has beautiful firm white flesh, similar to cod. To clarify butter, heat the butter in a deep pan until it boils, take off the heat and skim off the froth. Leave to settle for 10 minutes, then gently pour off the clear clarified butter, leaving the milky sediment behind.

SERVES 4

4 x 200g portions of ling, skin on
1 lemon, sliced
white wine
salt
cracked pepper
bay leaf and sprig of thyme

HOLLANDAISE SAUCE

4 egg yolks
1 tablespoon white wine vinegar
2 tablespoons water
250g butter, clarified
salt, white pepper
lemon juice

Cover the fish with cold water, add a slice or two of lemon, a splash of white wine, the seasoning and herbs. Quickly bring to the boil and immediately take off the heat, then leave to cook slowly for 10–15, minutes depending on the thickness of the fish.

For the hollandaise, put the egg yolks into a thick-based saucepan with the water and vinegar. Whisk over a very low heat, making sure all of the pan is scraped by the whisk. Gradually increase the heat so that the sauce emulsifies, becoming smooth and creamy. This should take 10–12 minutes. Do not over heat or the eggs will scramble. Take off the heat and, while still whisking, slowly pour in the clarified butter. Season with salt, pepper and lemon juice to taste. To make the sauce even richer, you could add a tablespoon or two of whipped cream.

TROUT WITH ALMONDS

SERVES 4

4 trout, about 250g each
100g plain flour
2 tablespoons cooking oil
120g butter
60g flaked almonds
juice of 1 lemon
salt, pepper

Snip the fins off the trout and remove the guts and gills. Rinse the fish under cold water and pat dry with kitchen towel. Dust in seasoned flour and place in a frying pan with the hot oil and 60g of frothing butter. Cook over moderate heat for 5 minutes each side until golden, basting with the butter all the time. Take off the heat, place the trout in a serving dish and leave to rest in a warm place.

Discard the cooking fat and cook the remaining butter over a high heat until frothy. Add the almonds, toss in the butter until golden, add the lemon juice and spoon over the trout.

Being a Roux 71

ARTICHOKES VINAIGRETTE

As a kid this was a real treat, but I remember my English friends coming round for dinner and being quite scared by this alien thing on a plate. I loved the sheer delight and fun of tearing off the leaves, dipping them into the vinaigrette, and finally drawing the leaf through clenched teeth to leave a morsel of deliciously deep-flavoured artichoke. When all the leaves have been chewed, only the heart and the inedible choke is left. This needs to be lifted or scraped out with a spoon. Add another drizzle of vinaigrette and one of the most classic and satisfying starters is complete.

SERVES 4

4 large globe artichokes
salt
1 lemon
VINAIGRETTE
25ml olive oil
75ml vegetable oil
2 teaspoons Dijon mustard
25ml white wine vinegar
salt, pepper

Snap the stems off the artichokes and place them in a deep pan. Cover with cold water, a little salt and the lemon cut into quarters. Bring to the boil and simmer gently for 30–40 minutes. You may need to put a plate on the artichokes to keep them submerged.

Take the artichokes out of the water and drain. Whisk all the vinaigrette ingredients together and serve with the artichokes. I think these are best served warm, but they can be refrigerated and eaten the next day.

VEAL TONGUE WITH SAUCE GRIBICHE

Offal has always been popular in the Roux household. The smell of simmering veal tongue usually meant two meals – hot tongue one day, then a rich vegetable broth made with the stock the day after.

SERVES 4

1 large veal tongue
1 carrot
2 sticks celery
1 medium onion, studded with 1 clove
1 clove garlic
1 bay leaf and a sprig of thyme
salt

SAUCE GRIBICHE

3 hard-boiled eggs
1 teaspoon Dijon mustard
salt, pepper
1 tablespoon white wine vinegar
220ml vegetable oil
2 tablespoons chopped herbs – chives, chervil, tarragon, parsley
1 tablespoon chopped gherkins
1 tablespoon fine capers

Rinse the tongue under a cold tap for 10 minutes. Place in a pan, cover generously with cold water and bring to the boil. Skim well, turn down the heat to a gentle simmer and add the vegetables, herbs and salt. Cook for 90 minutes or until tender when pricked with a kitchen fork. You may need to top up the liquid with boiling water.

To make the sauce, remove the yolks from the eggs and put them in a bowl with the mustard, salt, pepper and vinegar. Slowly whisk in the oil to emulsify like a mayonnaise. Finally mix in the herbs, gherkins, capers and chopped egg whites. Remove the tongue and peel away the skin while hot. Slice and serve with the sauce.

PASTA WITH CHICKEN LIVERS

Pasta is a regular staple throughout France. My family have always eaten pasta in various guises, with or without sauces. Quick to cook and filling – my idea of fast food.

SERVES 4

200g chicken livers
3 shallots
3 cloves garlic
1 tablespoon olive oil
60g butter
salt, pepper
2 tablespoons roughly chopped parsley
2 tablespoons Madeira
500g spaghetti or tagliatelle

Trim the livers and cut them into big chunks. Peel and chop the shallots and garlic. Heat the oil in a frying pan until it's smoking, season the livers and fry them until browned, but still very pink inside.

Add the butter, shallots and garlic to the pan and cook until the butter bubbles. Add the parsley and Madeira, simmer for a minute, then toss into the piping hot, freshly cooked pasta.

APPLE BEIGNETS

My family always fought over these beignets, which are best eaten straight out of the fryer and dusted with sugar. Careful, though – they're hot!

SERVES 4

4 apples (Cox, Granny Smith or Russet)
5g yeast
50ml warm milk
1 pinch salt
20g caster sugar
250ml lager
120g plain flour, sifted
flour for dusting
vegetable oil
sugar for dusting

Peel and core the apples, then slice them into doughnut-like rings, about 1cm thick. To make the batter, whisk the yeast into the warm milk to dissolve, then add the salt, sugar and lager, and finally the sifted flour. Cover and leave to rest for 20 minutes.

Heat the oil in a large pan. Dust the apples in a little flour, dip them in the batter, then gently drop into the hot oil. Cook for 2 or 3 minutes until golden and crisp on both sides. Drain and serve immediately. Crème fraîche, lightly sweetened and enhanced with a generous splash of Calvados, is a real treat with these.

THREE

The masters' apprentice

I decided to leave school at 16 and I talked to my father about going into the business with him. He recommended that I start my training with pastry, because it instils such discipline. Pastry making is a science – not like cooking, which can involve more than a little flair and ad libbing. With pastry, you've got to get it right. You've got to be very precise.

So off I went to Paris in September 1976 to start my apprenticeship under Maître Pâtissier Hellegouarche. In my view, and in the view of many others, he was the finest pastry chef in Paris, along with Jean Millet and Gaston Lenôtre. Hellegouarche was a very small, unique shop on rue Vaugirard, near Montparnasse. It was at the cutting-edge of French pâtisserie, so in many ways the place to be. If you wanted to be a pastry chef, it was one of the addresses where you had to work. It was a very special thing to be an apprentice there.

Every year Monsieur Hellegouarche took on two apprentices for two years. The first year of apprenticeship was really just cleaning and preparation work – peeling and chopping fruit, and washing up. That was your responsibility and everything had to be kept spotless at all times. You weren't given any kind of responsibility for cooking or finishing off a pastry or anything like that for a whole year. There were two second-year apprentices and they would help you along. There was a lot of camaraderie among the apprentices and it was very much all for one and one for all.

As well as working at the pastry shop, I had to go to catering college, which was in St Mandé. I liked it because there was a goal, and the goal was to pass the exam at the end and be a qualified pastry chef. Throughout the time of my apprenticeship, I spent three weeks of every month in the pastry shop and one week at college. We were taught French and mathematics, which seemed bizarre, but that was the way it had to be, because pastry is such a precise science. Then there was health and hygiene, pastry theory and practical science lessons. You were assessed on all that at the end of the two years and you took very rigorous exams. For me, it was difficult because I'd had an English education and being taught in French was not easy.

But I got through all of that and really enjoyed it. I passed very well. I remember exactly what I had to do in my exams. I had to make choux pastry – an éclair and a Paris-Brest, which is a classic choux pastry dessert. I also had to make a mocha cake with genoise and coffee butter cream, puff pastry, apple tart, brioche and fondant. It was all very basic, but you had to have a certain level of skill to get through and to earn your certificate – Le Certificate d'Aptitude Professionel.

It was only in the second year of the apprenticeship that you began to do things in the kitchen. Then you were allowed to start weighing out recipes and finish off desserts that were going to be put into the shop window. If you showed you were up to it, they would slowly let you in on the act. But you had to prove to your immediate superior and to your boss that you were capable.

The work was difficult and demanding, and it set me off in the right direction. Henri Hellegouarche was a wonderful boss. He was there first thing in the morning and last thing at night. He always led from the front. Sometimes we made mistakes – it happens – and he would get upset and shout a bit, but he never screamed or ranted and raved. It was very controlled. He was always in total command.

We used the best ingredients. He would go to the market himself and bring back the van filled with top-quality fruit, the best of everything. The shop was absolutely beautiful, marble everywhere, and Colette, his wife, would make sure all the girls in the shop wore spotless uniforms. She would line them up in the morning and check them from head to toe. She was always fresh from the hairdresser and immaculate herself, a typically elegant French matron, and she ran the front of house with complete precision.

As apprentices, we were only allowed to work ten hours a day, although that was severely stretched during the busy times of the year, especially before holidays and religious festivals – Epiphany, Easter, All Saints' Day, Remembrance Day, Christmas and New Year.

Each occasion had its own specialties. At Christmas we made everything and anything, but one special item was the bûche de Noël, the traditional Christmas log. We'd start making them some time in October and freeze the bases, then start taking them out on December 22nd to finish off and decorate to order. The classic bûche was made with butter cream and fairly rich, but we also made lighter, more modern versions with different types of mousse, and others containing ice cream or sorbet. Then there were all the petits fours and cakes. It was an unbelievable amount of work.

I remember working on Christmas Eve and Christmas Day. The shop opened on Christmas morning, of course, for people to come and buy their Christmas desserts. On Christmas Day we finished work at around 11am or lunchtime, cleaned down and off we went to celebrate. The two Christmases I was in Paris, I went to my Uncle Jean and Aunt Danielle for a late lunch. My maternal grandmother, Jacqueline, was there with Emile and there were family reunions with our cousins as well.

I was particularly fond of my Aunt Danielle and Uncle Jean, who was the sweetest man. When I was doing my apprenticeship in Paris between the ages of 16 and 18, I saw a lot of them. They were very kind and hospitable to me and one of my most precious memories is the time when later on in my life I was able to repay their kindness by inviting them to an old brasserie in Paris called L'Ami Louis. It still exists and it's in the Latin Quarter. I don't think the walls have been painted since the 1950s, so they're all nicotine stained. It's a small room in a quiet street. I still go there occasionally and even the taxi drivers sometimes get lost. The menu hasn't changed since day one. The service is almost brusque. The food is plonked onto the table. But you just can't fault it. Very, very expensive, but the best quality ingredients, cooked in the best possible way.

It used to have a Michelin star. My aunt and uncle had heard of it, but they'd never been there. I remember getting a very expensive bottle of wine as well and the look of happiness on Jean's face is something I'll never forget. I remember exactly what we ate. Foie gras to begin with. At L'Ami Louis they bring the terrine to the table

OPPOSITE: In the kitchens at Hellegouarche in Paris.

and you help yourself and eat it with toasted baguette. I had a pigeon and Jean had a kidney, roasted in its fat – a whole kidney brought to the table. I remember we had a whole sliced potato cake cooked in duck fat, and a confit de canard – it was half a duck. We're going back at least 25 years, but I can still remember the exact taste of every single dish.

The hours were even longer in my second year of apprenticeship. We would be there at 6 in the morning and finish whenever our work was completed in the evening.

I'll never forget it. We would work incredibly hard in the weeks leading up to Christmas, getting in at 4 in the morning and working until late in the evening. But that Christmas Eve, we finished work around 10 in the evening and Henri Hellegouarche came in and said, 'Look lads, I've prepared a dinner for you. Let's all sit down and have a glass of wine.' So the whole team – front of house and back of house – sat down together at a huge marble table and he got out the bottles of wine. I still remember it now: he'd prepared roast beef with various trimmings and we ate like kings for an hour or so.

Then he suddenly got up, looked at his watch and said, 'Right, see you in an hour.' And so we started again, at midnight on Christmas morning, and worked through the night. I had a room about five minutes away, so I went back there, crashed out for 20 minutes and then got up again. The others, who lived maybe 20 or 30 miles away, just went to the café next door, had a couple of coffees and came back. But there was not a word of complaint from anyone, nothing. It was normal.

And he was there as well, all night long. For me it was a learning curve, something that will stay in my memory forever. I remember being so shattered and then finishing work around noon and going home for a quick shower before having Christmas lunch with my family. I could just about keep my eyes open for the meal. And then on Boxing Day it was back to work again. It was quiet at first, but soon it was New Year and busy.

We used to have one and a half days off a week – Sunday afternoon and Monday, when the shop was closed. For the first couple of months I was living with my grandmother, Germaine. She had a tiny flat – just her bedroom, a dining room/ lounge, a tiny kitchen and a toilet. There was no bathroom. I lived on the sofa for two months until a bedsit, a little studio with a bathroom on the corridor, became free and I moved into that. It was very practical because it was only five minutes away from work.

But you can imagine – a 16 year old living on his own in Paris. Talk about burning the candle at both ends. I had great fun and went out every night to bars and nightclubs. You name it and I went there. Montparnasse is a fantastic area and there were a lot of Brittany bars there at the time that were really more like pubs than bars. They were rough, but good fun. I had a good group of friends from catering college and we met up regularly after work.

There was a wonderful Arab restaurant which made the best couscous I've ever tasted. I became friends with the son of the owner, a boy called Titif. Every time my mother came to Paris we'd go to eat the couscous, which was so good – merguez, the spicy Algerian sausage made with mutton and spices, loads of vegetables and home-made harissa scented with rose petals and roasted garlic. And pastilla – pigeon pie. You didn't sit at a table, but on floor cushions at low tables where great huge bowls of food were served.

Obviously if you're going out every night, you get tired and sometimes forget yourself in the morning, but M. Hellegouarche had novel ways of making you remember to be on time. I was late once or twice and he would scowl and give a warning. So I'd be a good boy for a couple of months and then I'd be late again. His punishment for being late was to make me peel almonds. Hellegouarche was one of the few places, even then, which made its own marzipan and he'd buy great sacks of almonds – 25-kilo sacks of raw almonds. They were shelled, but they still had their brown skins. You have to blanch them in boiling water to soften the skins and then pop the almonds out with your fingers. After a while, this becomes incredibly painful – and 25 kilos is a lot of almonds!

So on this occasion, once everyone had gone and the place had been cleaned down, he produced a sack of almonds. He didn't disappear. He just sat in his office doing his paperwork until I'd finished. After about an hour, you start getting pains in your thumb and the skin becomes sore. But after two or three hours, you actually start drawing blood and your thumb and forefinger are completely raw. But he wouldn't say stop until I had finished peeling every last almond.

It was my pride that made me continue until the bitter end. I took the punishment, because I felt that if I'd given up, he would have given up on me. I can quite safely say I was never late again. It's something I'll never forget. And even now, I hate being late. I'd rather be 15 minutes early than be late. I can almost picture the almonds and my fingers if I'm going to be late. It taught me a lesson I'll never forget.

But this didn't stop me going out. I just made sure I was at work on time the next morning.

I used to drink beer at a little bar, two doors down, a private, seedy bar, more of a hookers' den to be brutally honest. And the hooker who presided over everything was called Janine – she was so rough, I'm sure she was a man. I used to drop in for a couple of beers at the end of the night before going home for a quick shower and setting off for work again. I wouldn't want to do that now.

The apprentices liked to play jokes on each other. At the shop, we also made pâtés and various other savouries. Once they sent me out to the butcher down the road, with a big bag of onion skins because apparently they'd phoned up and asked for onion skins to use as colouring for andouille, the tripe sausage.

I'd seen before onions being burnt on the stove for colouring, so it didn't seem too weird an order. It seemed almost plausible.

So off I went, walked in and told the butchers I'd got the sack of onion peels for them. And they looked at me, deadpan, and said no, they didn't need them, but such and such a shop further down the road wanted the onion skins. And off I went again with this sack to the other butcher. Now this is one of the longest streets in Paris and all the butchers were in on the trick. I think I ended up going to about four shops until I realised they were having me on. So I dumped the sack of onion skins, walked back to work and as soon as I walked in, everyone just burst out laughing. You feel a right idiot. It's just a custom in kitchens that all the young apprentices get sent off to do something silly. We do it here sometimes – send them off to do an errand like that. It's harmless fun.

Apprenticeship was just bliss for me – away from the constraints of living at home – and Paris was wonderful. I had my own digs but the safety of family there if I wanted it. I was independent. And I was doing what I wanted to do. It was fantastic. I worked extremely hard and learned a phenomenal amount.

It's a good idea for a young chef to learn pastry first and then go on to other areas of cooking. It teaches discipline, as you have to weigh everything properly. There are a lot of aspects of pastry work that can then be used elsewhere in the kitchen. You can't be slapdash. There are no short cuts in pastry. M. Hellegouarche never used anything ready mixed, like powdered custards. He would buy the best eggs to make custard properly and buy the best butter. And the pastry was always light. Pastry doesn't have to be stodgy if it's made properly to the correct recipe.

All the great desserts were in that shop – éclairs, petits fours, amandines and mille-feuilles, the classic puff pastry dessert. I remember when I was allowed to glaze my first mille-feuille, which was such a big thing. For weeks and weeks, I was shown how to temper the fondant and do the feathering on top, and then how to cut it. I had to bring my mille-feuille to Mme Hellegouarche for her to cast her eye over and approve. She knew that I had made it and then I was allowed to put it in the shop window. When I left the shop in the afternoon, I looked in the window and said to myself, 'I made that.' It was a good feeling.

But it was hard strenuous work. The ovens were enormous and you had to be strong to lift the huge, heavy baking trays in and out. I learned how to make and roll croissants and how to bake macaroons and all the charlottes. And I remember for May 1, Labour Day, we used to make little chocolate pots filled with different mousses. We'd spend ages making little sprigs of lily of the valley from icing sugar to decorate them. Each one took hours and hours so we made them weeks ahead. And then on May 1, the shop would be filled with these little chocolate pots with their sugar sprigs of lily of the valley.

Each religious festival had its own special cake. For the Epiphany, on January 6, it was the galette des rois. We'd make thousands of them. I remember being allowed to score the pastry for the first time... the thrill of it.

I loved my time at Hellegouarche, but I don't really have a sweet tooth. I do appreciate sweet things, but not overly sweet. I've never gone for confectionery, especially cheap confectionery. I can't stand it and I can't understand how people can eat those things. Whenever I go to Paris and drive past the shop, I get a wonderful warm feeling. It's still a pastry shop, but no longer owned by Henri Hellegouarche. Pierre Hermé has taken it on.

After my years with Hellegouarche, I spent some time in the family businesses. As well as Le Gavroche, there was Le Gamin and Le Poulbot. I went back to work as a chef in Le Poulbot, the restaurant where I used to wash dishes when I was 13. We used to sell 60 omelettes an hour and we had only two frying pans to cook them in. We had great buckets of eggs and huge mountains of chips all ready to go in the kitchen and from 12.30 until 2pm it was a fast and furious rush. The kitchen was in the basement and the orders were pegged onto a string which came down from the restaurant. We'd cook as fast as we could and then we hauled the food up by hand in a dumb waiter to the dining room. That was tough work.

Then I went to work for Alain Chapel in Mionnay, near Lyon. At the time, he was the person to work for. If you were a young aspiring chef, that was the place to be. Alain Chapel's was the definitive three-star Michelin restaurant. Young chefs wanted to work there because of his philosophy of cooking and his style. The philosophy was new, but nonetheless very classical, simple and straightforward – nothing was allowed to mask the ingredients and there were no arguments between flavours. Everything was allowed to speak for itself and was cooked as perfectly as humanly possible.

RICH BRIOCHE

MAKES 1 LARGE LOAF OR 30 SMALL BUNS
15g fresh baker's yeast
500g plain flour, sifted
6 eggs
2 teaspoons salt
50g sugar
300g butter, room temperature
beaten egg

Place the yeast in the bottom of a KitchenAid bowl with a few drops of water to soften it. Add the sifted flour, the eggs one at a time, and the salt and sugar to the yeast and slowly knead together with the dough hook attachment. (You can do this by hand but it's actually better when kneaded by machine.)

After 5 minutes the dough should be smooth and elastic. Add the softened butter and continue to knead at a slightly faster speed for 10 minutes. Make sure all the butter is well incorporated. Put the dough in a large clean container, cover with clingfilm and refrigerate for 12 hours. After 4 hours, knock the dough down by punching it firmly to release the fermentation gases.

Preheat the oven to 200°C/Gas 6. When ready to cook the brioche, tip the dough out onto a floured surface and make into balls or roll into loaf tins. Leave in a warm, draught-free place until risen by one-third, then brush with beaten egg and cook until golden. A loaf will need about 40 minutes and individual brioche about 15 minutes.

CHOUX BUNS 'SALAMBO'

CHOUX PASTRY	CRÈME PÂTISSIÈRE
125ml water	1 vanilla pod
125ml milk	250ml milk
1 pinch salt	4 yolks
1 teaspoon sugar	65g caster sugar
100g butter	30g plain flour
150g plain flour, sifted	1 large shot of Kirsch
4 eggs	200g caster sugar for caramel

First make the choux pastry. Put the water, milk, salt, sugar and butter in a pan over high heat and bring to the boil. Take off the heat and beat in the sifted flour using a spatula. When the mixture is smooth, put it back on the heat and beat vigorously for one minute. Tip this paste into a bowl and beat in the eggs one at a time. Now put the paste into a piping bag with a 1.5cm nozzle, and pipe out buns measuring about 3cm across onto a non-stick baking sheet. Cook in a preheated oven at 220°C/Gas 7 for 5 minutes. Open the door for a few seconds to let out the steam, then turn it down to 180°C/Gas 4 for 20 minutes or until the buns are fully cooked.

For the crème patissière
Split the vanilla pod, scrape out the seeds and add them to the milk along with the pod. Bring to the boil. Whisk the yolks and sugar until pale, then add the flour. Pour the boiling milk onto the egg yolk mixture and mix well. Pour back into the pan and bring to the boil, stirring well with a whisk as the mixture will thicken and can burn easily. Take off the heat and place in a bowl. Cover and chill. When needed, whisk in the Kirsch.

Make a little hole in the base of each choux bun and fill with the flavoured cream. To finish the buns, make a caramel by cooking the 200 sugar over a high heat until it is golden brown. Carefully dip the round side of each bun into the caramel.

CROISSANTS

MAKES 30 SMALL

45g fresh yeast
400g warm water
40g milk powder
800g flour, sifted
80g sugar

20g salt
40g butter, melted
300g butter, room temperature
beaten egg

Dissolve the yeast in the warm water and milk powder. Add to the sifted flour, sugar, salt and the 40g of melted butter. Knead well by hand or machine for 4–5 minutes until smooth and everything is incorporated, but do not overwork. Cover and leave to rise until doubled in size.

Roll the dough out to A4 size. Place the softened butter in the middle and fold over all the edges of the dough to envelope it completely. Dust with flour and gently roll out to a rectangle about 40 x 26cm. Take both ends, fold them to the centre and fold again to make a much smaller rectangle. Wrap in clingfilm and refrigerate for an hour. Then repeat the process of rolling out and folding the dough.

Roll out the dough on a floured surface to a thickness of 1cm and cut triangles with a base of 12cm. Roll these triangles towards the point, then bring the points together to form the croissant shape. Place the croissants on a baking tray and leave them to rise for about 20 minutes.

Brush with beaten egg and bake in a hot oven at 180°C/Gas 4 until cooked. The croissants can be frozen, once rolled, and taken out of the freezer an hour before cooking.

CHOCOLATE MOUSSE MIONNAY

One of my favourite desserts, this was always on the huge dessert tray at Alain Chapel. It's simple, and because it has very little sugar and no cream the real taste of chocolate shines through.

SERVES 8

330g of the finest bitter chocolate available
(70% cacao solids is ideal and Amadei make
some beautiful single-estate chocolate that
is quite simply the best)
30g butter, room temperature
8 egg whites
1 tablespoon caster sugar
8 egg yolks

Melt the chocolate in a double boiler or in the microwave. Do not overheat. Beat in the soft butter.

Whisk the egg whites until frothy, then add the sugar and continue to whisk until firm. Stir the yolks into the chocolate mixture, and then fold in the egg whites. Do not over mix. Pour the mousse into individual glasses or a big serving bowl and chill for at least 6 hours.

SPICED CHERRIES IN KRIEK BEER

SERVES 6–8
1 litre Kriek beer (cherry-flavoured Belgian beer)
2 vanilla pods, split in half lengthways
1 stick of cinnamon
5 star anise
juice of 1 lemon and 1 orange
grated zest of ½ lemon and ½ orange
½ tablespoon chopped root ginger
300g light brown sugar
1.5kg cherries, stoned
3 tablespoons Kirsch

Bring all the ingredients, except the cherries and Kirsch, to the boil. Then add the cherries, cover and simmer for 2–3 minutes. Leave to cool.

The cherries are delicious cold or warm, but they are even better if kept refrigerated for 24 hours before using. Add the Kirsch just before you serve them.

PINK PRALINE TART

Pink pralines, sugar-coated almonds, are a speciality of Lyon and perfect for this tart. If you can't find the pink ones you can use brown pralines instead.

SERVES 6–8
SWEET PASTRY
120g butter, cold
120g caster sugar
2 egg yolks
1 tablespoon crème fraîche
250g plain flour, sifted
PRALINE MIX
300g pink pralines
300g double cream

First make the pastry. Gently rub together the butter and sugar, then add the yolks and crème fraîche. Bring the paste together with the sifted flour. Wrap the pastry in clingfilm and refrigerate for at least 2 hours.

Press the pastry into a 24cm flan ring and cover with a piece of greaseproof paper weighed down with beans. Cook fully in a preheated oven at 180°C /Gas 4 – this will take about 20 minutes. Remove the beans and paper and cook for a further 5–6 minutes.

Crush the pralines with a rolling pin then put in a pan with the cream. Boil until it reaches 104°C on the thermometer. Pour this mixture into the cooked tart base. Leave to cool before cutting.

TARTE AUX POMMES
FRENCH APPLE TART

SERVES 4

200g puff pastry (good-quality bought pastry is fine)
2 tablespoons apple compote
4 apples (Cox or Granny Smith)
2 tablespoons caster sugar
1 tablespoon butter
beaten egg

Roll out the puff pastry on a floured surface to dinner plate size. Cut to a perfect circle and pinch over the edges. Turn the pastry over and lay on a non-stick baking tray. (Turning puff pastry after rolling or cutting helps the layers to rise successfully.)

Preheat the oven to 200°C/Gas 6. Dock the pastry all over with a fork and smear on the apple compote, leaving a gap of 1cm around the edges. Peel, core and halve the apples, then slice them thinly. Starting on the edge, overlap the slices onto the apple compote, fanning them out in a circular fashion and gradually coming to the centre. The apples should look like an even spiral.

Brush the apples with melted butter and sprinkle with caster sugar. Brush the edges of the tart with beaten egg. Bake in the preheated oven for 10 minutes, then turn down to 180°C/Gas 4 for a further 20 minutes. The tart should be cooked though and lightly caramelised on the top.

Best served warm with a little crème fraîche. If serving the tart cold, brush the top with a little warmed apricot jam or apple jelly to give it a lovely shine.

Alain Chapel's restaurant at Mionnay was very beautiful and had a number of bedrooms as well where guests could stay. In the centre was a large courtyard with a wonderful garden, which Monsieur Chapel looked after himself. Although it was one of the best restaurants in France, it was still a family house and a family business. He was very much hands on – checking the rooms, the waiters, the cleanliness of everything – and he went to the markets himself for all the fruit and vegetables. He was there all the time. So were his wife, Madame Suzanne Chapel, and his mother, who worked behind the cash desk.

Mionnay was a tiny little village with nothing much else in it other than the restaurant. People came from all over the world – it was a gastronomic pilgrimage for them. Although the country around Lyon is pretty, it isn't spectacular, so the restaurant and hotel were very much the main attraction. There was a post office, a café, a church, and a few houses. That was it. It's still much the same and the restaurant still exists, although Alain Chapel died in 1990. He was an extraordinary chef, an inspiration and very formidable. In all the time I worked for him, I never called him by his first name. I would not have dared. It was always Monsieur Chapel or Chef if we were in the kitchen.

I was completely terrified and quaking in my boots when I first met him and his first wife Danielle. My parents and I had come over from England to talk about me working at the restaurant, and when I might start. The five of us met in a restaurant called Chez Bérard in the next village along from Mionnay. It was run by Marc and Marlyse Beaujeu, who were ex-employees of Le Gavroche. They'd gone back to France and decided to open their own restaurant, so it was very nice to see some familiar faces.

We had lunch there – a very simple lunch, but delicious. I wasn't so nervous that I can't remember what we ate. We had a Lyonnaise salad – poached egg and thick, crisp lardons with frisée and dandelion leaves and a red wine vinegar dressing. And lots of wonderful fresh bread, of course. We also had faiselle, which I love. It's a very fresh curd cheese, made from either goat's or cow's milk

Feb – Avil. 80

navets noirs confits et escalope de foie gras de canard chaud

crème d'asperges vertes et brocoli
petit ragoût et blancs de volailles en chartreuse

ou filet de carpeau au poivre et à la moëlle,
sa garniture de quenelles et fanes de légumes

ou ragoût de coquilles st-jacques,
d'huitres de pleine mer aux poireaux et truffes noires

gâteau de foies blonds de poularde de bresse
baigné d'une sauce aux queues d'écrevisses

ou poulette de bresse en vessie, les petits légumes nouveaux, sauce albufera

ou chausson de canard et filet de veau, son beurre
petite salade mélangée aux cœurs de canards et huile d'olives

quelques fromages fermiers

desserts glacés, mignardises, bugnes,
pralines, candis et chocolats
pâtisserie maison

225

possibilité du choix de deux plats : 195

A typical Chapel menu from the time I worked at the restaurant.

with a texture similar to mascarpone. This one was seasoned with crème fraîche, herbs, garlic, red wine vinegar and olive oil.

My parents and M. and Mme Chapel arranged that I should serve a further apprenticeship there. I got myself some digs in the village opposite the restaurant, bought a clapped-out white Peugeot to get me from A to B – I think my family specialises in clapped-out cars – and began work. For me, this was the best opportunity I could possibly have had.

Chapel was way ahead of other restaurateurs at the time in combining the cooking of East and West. He was working with the famous Japanese cookery school, the Tsuji Culinary Institute, and was already looking at opening a restaurant in Japan. Only Gaston Lenôtre and Roger Vergé were doing that sort of thing, so Chapel was really one of the pioneers.

Chapel also used oriental ingredients like ginger and five-spice in a way no one else was doing then. One of the fish dishes on the menu was gilthead bream with a sweet red wine reduction sauce, and he served it with a garnish of ginger and soy sauce – 'crêpe Japonaise'. That was very unusual for those days, very avant garde. It was something that would take you aback. You'd taste it and know immediately it was something new and exciting.

The British often joke about the French not knowing how to use spices, and they harp on about the British Empire and its great spice trade heritage. Well, it's just not true – the French do understand spices very well, and they were equally important spice traders. French cooks have used spices throughout history. Just because there are no curry houses in France doesn't mean that the French do not appreciate spices.

Cooking with spices and chillies

I love chillies of all kinds, from the tiny fierce bird's-eye chillies to jalapeños. I also use wonderfully fragrant chillies called *espelettes* after the place they come from in southwest France. You can use them fresh or dried and they give a wonderful warmth without burning. I like using powdered chilli to sprinkle on dishes as well.

In the south of France we do cook with chillies quite a bit. Most of the varieties we like are moderately hot, although we do have a variety like bird's-eye, which is very fiery. My mother-in-law uses these all the time in her stews. Further north, they don't like chillies and rarely use them.

You do need to use chillies with caution, particularly in a first course, otherwise your palate can be ruined for the rest of the meal. And chillies can be a disaster if a fine wine is being served. I love going to the Seychelles, and in bars and hotels the waiters always put out dishes of pureed chilli for people who like it. And they always serve chilli at breakfast as well. You see all these people queuing up for breakfast and they see a bowl of what they think is a relish. And then you see their faces after they've taken a mouthful!

Other spices such as ginger and cumin also have their place in French cuisine. People often forget that France had a flourishing spice trade and had huge colonies all over Africa, the West Indies and the Indian Ocean. Spices were traded and used extensively. Classic cuisine in the Escoffier style only used spices sparingly, but they were always part of our heritage.

To me the most invaluable spice is pepper, not just white or black, but every type of pepper. They're all fragrant and all have different flavour notes.

SCALLOPS WITH FIVE-SPICE SAUCE

This five-spice sauce works well with scallops or with oily fish,
such as red mullet or mackerel.

SERVES 4

500ml strong red wine
1 tablespoon five-spice powder
1 tablespoon caster sugar
1 tablespoon sherry vinegar
300ml veal stock (see p. 303)
12 fresh, extra-large, diver-caught scallops
olive oil
2 tablespoons butter
salt

Boil the red wine until it is reduced by half. In another pan, over
moderate heat, warm the spice until it releases a strong aroma, then
add the sugar and vinegar. Cook for another 2–3 minutes, then add
the wine and stock. Simmer until the sauce coats the back of a spoon,
then pass it through a fine sieve. Season and whisk in the cold butter
to thicken and shine the sauce. It may need a little more sugar,
depending on the acidity of the red wine.

Sear the seasoned scallops in a non-stick pan with a tiny drizzle of
olive oil. The scallops should be caramelised on one side, and slightly
undercooked, otherwise they will be chewy.

Arrange the scallops on the plate with a little sauce and serve with
fried vegetable crisps or buttered noodles.

Of course, despite his interest in Japanese and other cuisines, Chapel still cooked the classical dishes typical of his region. Two of the most popular items on his menu were the poulet de Bresse – stuffed with truffles, wrapped up in a pig's bladder and poached – and stuffed calves' ears with fried parsley. He cooked a wonderful hot chicken liver mousse as well, something that I have on the menu at Le Gavroche because it is particularly good.

He had another dish which was on the menu for a while, chicken tripe. It was an incredibly difficult, fiddly thing to prepare. First of all, the tripe had to be delivered warm, so we had to get it minutes after the hen had been killed. And then it had to be blanched within the hour. We used to get these bags of warm chicken innards

Alain Chapel's warm chicken liver parfait
SERVES 6

180g chicken livers (not dark), trimmed
60g beef marrow, rinsed
500ml milk
100ml single cream
4 whole eggs
2 egg yolks
1 clove garlic
1 sprig thyme
salt, pepper, grated nutmeg

Put all the ingredients in a food blender and blitz until smooth. Press though a fine sieve. Check seasoning and pour into well-buttered ramekin moulds. Cover with buttered foil and poach in a water bath in an oven at 120°C/Gas ½ for 30 minutes or until set. Leave to rest for a few minutes before turning out. Garnish with a crayfish claw.

that had to be cooked immediately and then put into earthenware pots. This dish wasn't on the menu for long, thankfully.

M. Chapel respected and paid homage to local ingredients, such as truffles, carp, crayfish and frogs' legs. We used to get the frogs live, which you would never see now. They were proper wild frogs, caught by the postman with nets or a trap, and they arrived in huge hessian sacks. We had to dispatch them with a pair of scissors, then skin them – not a nice job to say the least.

When I started, I didn't have that much experience in the kitchen, so Alain Chapel put me in the pastry section. This was a perfect way for me to get to know the restaurant and that's where I stayed for the first year.

I worked under a man called Janot who'd been there in the pastry section since day one. He was part of the furniture and I learned so much from him. What a character! He used to smoke a brand of French cigarettes called Boyard. They are probably about ten times stronger than Gitanes, with the same black tobacco. But these were rolled in maize paper, which made them even stronger and smellier. I'm sure he got out of bed with one of these in his mouth. You'd have a conversation with him, and the cigarette would just be stuck to his lip, very often not even lit but it would always be there. What astounded me was that he'd actually be smoking while he was working. Janot had a massive motor bike and wore all the leather gear. But even when he was wearing his crash helmet, he would still have a fag hanging out of his mouth.

Alain Chapel was also famous for his huge silver dessert platter where there would be about 12 different desserts of the region – gâteau aux noix, oeufs à la neige, tarte aux pralines, things like that. They would be made fresh for lunch and for dinner and put on the platter and sent out. The majority of people eating in the restaurant would choose their dessert from this massive tray of pastries. Occasionally we'd get other orders for something from the à la carte, such as pear soufflé or the like, but that was unusual.

We'd also make all our own brioche and croissants to serve at breakfast for the guests in the rooms. It was a very small pastry department – Janot, myself and an apprentice, and we got through a lot of work. One of the great things I saw there, and haven't seen anywhere since, was Janot making the restaurant's own little bon-bon liqueurs. Janot would boil up syrup to a certain, very precise degree and then add the liqueur. We took these little wooden trays – there were perhaps 20 or 30 of them – and filled them with cornflour, which had to be very carefully sifted. That was my job. Little imprints were made in the cornflour and the liqueur syrup carefully poured into each one. They would be covered again with sifted cornflour and left to dry overnight. Then you had to turn the liqueurs very delicately while they were still in the cornflour and leave them again for 24 or 36 hours. After that, you had to brush off the excess cornflour very delicately with a silk brush and leave them on a rack to dry further.

After a week's work, the end result was a batch of bon-bons with perfectly crystallised, hard and crunchy exteriors that you bit into to discover a liquid interior – absolutely beautiful and delicious. These were served as part of the petits fours. But they were incredibly time-consuming to make and we always lost a few along the way because they were so fragile. They're something I'll never see again because they were just too labour-intensive to be worthwhile. Now it's all done mechanically in factories.

I started at Alain Chapel at the same time as Ghert Van-Heche who is still a great friend. Ghert was in the cold preparation area – salads – and we hit it off straight away. We had digs in the same house and invariably went out together whenever we could. He was a big beer drinker as well, and we both enjoyed the night life of Lyon, which was only half an hour's drive away. We were always playing tricks. One day we put live eels in the beds of the kitchen porters and of course they went straight to M. Chapel. He rounded us up and gave us a big lecture.

But he rounded on them as well when they started to roast hedgehogs – a North African delicacy – on the pavement outside the restaurant. Can you imagine? A bloody great bonfire with a roasting hedgehog on top, right outside a three-star restaurant!

An evening out with my great friend Ghert Van-Heche.

Although we wouldn't dare to speak out against M. Chapel in any way, that didn't stop us playing tricks on him, too, with the Labrador dog my father and mother had brought over from England for him. He'd really wanted one. My parents had brought Labradors over for Jean Troisgros, Paul Bocuse and Gaston Lenôtre as well. At one stage it seemed every three-star Michelin chef had a Labrador from the Roux family.

M. Chapel's Labrador was called Nemo, and he was a lovely, playful dog. In the courtyard, there was a fountain where we used to keep carp and crayfish. Every time Nemo walked past, we would throw little titbits into the fountain and the dog would dive in. The next thing you would hear would be M. Chapel shouting and screaming at the dog to get out of the fountain. Of course, the dog would get a bollocking and we would roar with laughter.

They were the light moments. Most of the time, for the first few months at least, it was very nerve-wracking to work in a three-star restaurant and M. Chapel was quite scary. He was a big guy. He rarely shouted or screamed, but if he said something, you sure knew about it. We all had a lot of respect for him, not through fear but because he really was awe-inspiring.

The main team comprised Guy Gateau, the chef de cuisine; Robert Duffault, a sous-chef; André Barcet; a Japanese chef de partie called Kami Kakimoto, who is now a famous chef in Japan; Ghert and myself. The restaurant sat 60, but in summer months, you could push that up to 80 because people could eat on the terrace.

It was a wonderful experience. We had Sunday night and Monday off, although I remember we used to open on Sunday nights as well in summer. In the second year, I moved into the kitchen and worked with Ghert on the cold section and salads, preparing the famous salade d'homard which is still on the menu over there. It contained warm lobster, a vinaigrette made with the lobster coral and juices, tarragon mustard, red wine vinegar and olive oil, York ham, pieces of poached pigeon, sourdough croutons rubbed with garlic, and mesclun salad mixed with bitter leaves. It was served in a big dish,

Alain Chapel's mushroom and artichoke salad

SERVES 2

60g raw mushrooms (wild or cultivated)
2 baby artichokes, trimmed of the
  spiny leaves
30g fresh black truffle (optional)
juice of ½ lemon
1 tablespoon truffle juice
3 tablespoons extra virgin olive oil
salt, freshly ground pepper
1 tablespoon picked chervil and chives

Clean and thinly slice the mushrooms and artichokes, and slice the truffle if using. Mix the dressing with a spoon and dress the salad at the very last second, just before serving.

Alain Chapel's lobster salad dressing

FOR 2 LOBSTER SALADS

lobster juices and coral
2 tablespoons cooking court bouillon
2 teaspoons tarragon mustard
1 tablespoon red wine vinegar
4 tablespoons extra virgin olive oil
salt, pepper

Take the head off the cooked lobster over a bowl to collect the juices and coral. Use a small spoon to coax it all out. Add the court bouillon and into this whisk the tarragon mustard, red wine vinegar and extra virgin olive oil. Season with salt and pepper. Use to dress a lobster salad.

tossed in front of the customer and then put on the plate. There were no fancy decorations, but it was a beautiful salad. I put it on here sometimes as a special and I mention M. Chapel, of course.

Then there was a pigeon jelly and hand-raised pâtés made in wonderful old moulds, all sliced in front of the customer in the restaurant – there was a lot of carving in front of the diners.

Everything was chopped by hand. There were no machines anywhere. All egg whites were whisked by hand. Everything was done by hand. These pâtés were made twice a week, again by hand. M. Chapel believed they tasted better like that. I remember once I weighed out and milled some pepper, thinking I would get ahead before the restaurant got very busy. M. Chapel came in to supervise and saw that I'd milled 15 grams of fresh pepper. He asked why I'd done this, and I explained it was to get ahead, but I got such a bollocking and he chucked all the pepper in the bin. It had to be freshly milled, not even half an hour old. That's how much of a perfectionist he was.

When M. Chapel was working on his first book I was required to make the pigeon jelly, one of his signature dishes, for the photographer. The pigeon jelly was made from the poaching broth of the pigeon breasts, clarified and set with gelatine, then served with a salad of baby leaves, carrots, chicken oysters, a bit of olive oil and some red wine vinegar. On the plate it looked like a rock garden and very beautiful. It was also featured on the tasting menu so it was a big, big seller.

It was summer and a warm day when the photographer was there, so I thought I'd be very clever and put in a couple of extra leaves of gelatine to make the jelly hold better for the photograph. I didn't overdo it, but M. Chapel immediately looked at the dish and said it wasn't as normal. I explained what I'd done and it went straight in the bin. For him, it had to be the exact same recipe, no matter how long it took the photographer to get the picture.

There were a lot of things like that in the restaurant that I'll never forget. All salads were dressed at the very last second. Nothing was pre-prepared and every dish had to be perfect.

Salads

Dressing a salad is a great test for any chef. Give them a bowl of leaves, a choice of vinegars and oils, and see what they do with it. Can they dress it properly? Can they season it properly? Which oils and vinegars will they choose?

I always dress a salad individually and I check all the salads that leave the kitchen. Salads are not just leaves. A salad dressing should bring out the flavour of the leaves and not drown them.

With rocket, for me it has to be olive oil, balsamic vinegar, salt and pepper, and absolutely nothing else. If you have a hard, bitter leaf, such as endive, you need something a little richer which will cling to the leaf, possibly with a hint of sweetness, from honey or sweet mustard. I wouldn't use a balsamic vinegar here, but orange or lemon juice, white wine vinegar or tarragon vinegar, with perhaps a little crème fraîche added.

I believe every leaf is different. Mâche, for example, is very delicate and is best served on its own, with just some good walnut oil and salt and pepper – little or no vinegar. Other soft leaves, such as mesclun and baby spinach, can also be prepared that way.

Radicchio, like endive, is available all year round now, which I think is a shame because they are winter leaves. Like batavia and escarole, these leaves are best eaten after a frost and then they are really crunchy and tasty. I don't like iceberg lettuce. It's tasteless. If you want a crunchy lettuce, cos is delicious. It has a hint of sweetness and goes well with a traditional French vinaigrette.

A salad can be ruined by a bad choice of vinaigrette, by being dressed an hour before you eat it, or being badly tossed so that one leaf is covered in dressing and the next leaf has none at all. I hate salads tossed by hand. There is no need to get your hands in the bowl. There are tongs and there are forks. Let's do it properly.

This autumn at the restaurant we've got a salad of root vegetables dressed with almond oil and a touch of raspberry vinegar. It's wonderful – very delicate and light.

SALADE LYONNAISE

The classic salade Lyonnaise should be made with dandelion leaves, but they can be a little bitter for some people. If you are lucky enough to have a garden with untreated areas in it, you can pick your own leaves. Alternatively, use frisée salad, also called curly endive.

SERVES 4

400g dandelion leaves or frisée salad
180g smoked streaky bacon
4 tablespoons olive oil
white wine vinegar
20 thin slices of small baguette bread
2 cloves garlic
4 free-range eggs
2 tablespoons red wine vinegar
salt and pepper

Pick, wash and dry the salad leaves. Cut the bacon into strips or batons, place them in a non-stick pan with a drop of olive oil and cook slowly over medium heat. Put a saucepan of water on to boil with a generous splash of white wine vinegar. Bake the baguette slices in a warm oven until dry and crisp, then rub with the cut garlic.

Crack the eggs and carefully drop them into the simmering, vinegared water to poach. The eggs should take about 4 minutes for the whites to be cooked, yet the yolk still very runny. Pour the golden-brown bacon and fat onto the salad with the bread, vinegar and remaining olive oil. Season lightly with salt but generously with pepper, toss and place the drained, hot eggs on top.

ENDIVE AND SALAD CREAM

SERVES 4

6 endives (3 red and 3 yellow)
1 tablespoon caster sugar
2 tablespoons malt vinegar
salt
2 teaspoons Coleman's English mustard
100ml single cream
pepper
flat-leaf parsley

Cut the endives in half lengthways and cut each half into 5 wedges. Make the dressing by whisking the sugar, vinegar, salt and mustard together, then add the cream and a little pepper.

Gently toss the pieces of endive in a little of the dressing and neatly place them on a plate or bowl. Drizzle with the remaining dressing and sprinkle with some washed and roughly chopped flat-leaf parsley.

ARTICHOKE AND PARMESAN SALAD

SERVES 4

12 baby artichokes (poivrade or épineux)
4 tablespoons strong olive oil
juice of 1 lemon
coarse sea salt, pepper
1 shallot
fresh basil leaves
80g Parmesan shavings

Using a small, very sharp knife, remove the outer leaves of each artichoke and peel the stalk. Cut off the top to reveal only the tender leaves and cut the stalk to about 3cm long. Using a very sharp vegetable slicer, slice as thinly as possible.

Lay the slices out on large plates, drizzle with the olive oil and lemon juice, then season. Sprinkle with the thinly sliced shallot, basil leaves and finally the Parmesan shavings. This must be served immediately to be at its best.

Some of the team at Alain Chapel – myself, Christian, Ghert and André.

The foie gras terrine at Alain Chapel was garnished with a salad of raw artichokes, mushrooms, shallots, chervil and fresh raw truffle. You'd slice all the ingredients, put them on a plate, and season with salt and pepper, olive oil, red wine vinegar and a little bit of truffle jus. It would be mixed with a fork, the seasoning would be rectified and then it would be placed on the plate.

Even if you had ten salads on order, you didn't dress them in one big bowl. You had to dress ten individual salads and each vinaigrette would be made to order. M. Chapel would check each one. You could not make a big bowl of vinaigrette beforehand. Each salad had to be made and dressed to taste. That's a major fault of a lot of chefs today. They won't taste anything. I'm always harping on to chefs and asking, 'Have you tasted it?' Invariably they haven't.

After the salad section, I worked on the fish section, but I was not allowed to cook fish for main courses, just to do garnishes and preparation. Only the chef de partie was allowed to cook. But I was allowed to cook the aperitifs – tiny little gudgeon, loach or perch, dipped in seasoned flour and deep fried to order and served with deep-fried parsley.

There was a great camaraderie there during those two years and we'd invariably go out together as a team. On nights off, we'd drive to Lyon together and sit down at one of several restaurants that were open all through the night. We'd have a grilled entrecôte or andouillete, something special to the region. We'd have a couple of bottles of wine and drive back at 3 or 4 in the morning. After a couple of hours' sleep, we'd go back to work and think nothing of it. It wasn't all beer in bars, although Ghert did introduce me to better beers, in particular Rodenbach beer, which is made by Trappist monks. Great friendships were made and continue to this day.

Once a month we made a point of going to a good bistro or a Michelin-starred restaurant, and working our way through the taster menu. We would drive for hours to sample other great restaurants in the area – La Tour Rose, a 15th-century hotel right in the middle of Lyon, and Leon de Lyon were just two of them. We weren't just hungry for food, we were hungry to learn and taste. We wanted to taste the best food and then to produce it ourselves.

When I turned 20, my father and mother flew down to meet me and we went to eat at Paul Bocuse's restaurant. I had the sea bass en croûte, one of his signature dishes. It was a wonderful meal.

Classic French vinaigrette
ENOUGH TO DRESS SALAD FOR 12

2 tablespoons white wine vinegar
2 teaspoons Dijon mustard
salt, pepper
6 tablespoons olive oil
1 shallot, finely chopped

Place the vinegar, mustard, salt and pepper in a bowl and whisk. Add the oil slowly and combine well. Mix in the shallot and the vinaigrette is ready to serve.

Offal

Tripe really is delicious and yes, I do eat it myself. So is andouillete or tripe sausage. An acquired taste maybe, but nonetheless delicious. It's something we don't see in England very much any more, and I don't put it on the menu at Le Gavroche because it wouldn't sell. We don't see much of brains either, something which rarely appears on the menu because again, it doesn't sell. I'm not a great fan, but Gisele loves them. Brains need acidity – lemons, capers or something like that – and they need to be fried.

I think kidneys, particularly veal kidneys, are completely delicious. They're not too strong in flavour, they're nice and chewy and they are particularly good with a cream and mustard sauce, which is how we serve them at Le Gavroche. They are very popular. And we keep all the fat and render that down for frying.

Lamb kidneys are very nice but they have to be new season's. Once they get old, they become too pungent and fatty. Veal liver is absolutely delicious and tender. Again, it can take stronger flavours like bacon, onions and sage. Heart? I'm not a great fan and I do find the texture a bit odd, although braised ox heart is one of my father's and my uncle's favourite dishes. Duck hearts, chicken hearts and livers are wonderful, but I'm not keen on pigs' liver. I find the flavour too strong.

Veal and lamb sweetbreads need to be blanched first. If you try to cook them from raw, you never get that wonderful creamy texture. They tend to be chewy if undercooked. Here, we poach them first in water with some vinegar and salt, then trim them up, dust them in flour and pan fry them. That way, they are crisp on the outside and creamy on the inside – expensive but delicious.

VEAL SWEETBREADS WITH APPLE

SERVES 4

800g–1kg veal sweetbreads
1 tablespoon white wine vinegar
2 Cox's apples
2 tablespoons Calvados
2 tablespoons butter
3 shallots, chopped
250ml dry cider
500ml veal stock (see p. 303)
flour for dredging
1 tablespoon olive oil
1 small sprig of rosemary
salt, pepper

Put the sweetbreads in a pan and cover with cold water. Add salt and the vinegar, quickly bring to the boil and simmer for 5 minutes. Leave to cool.

While the sweetbreads cool, make the sauce. Peel the apples and cut into very small dice – keep the peel and trimmings. Douse the dice with the Calvados. Sweat the peel and trimmings in a little of the butter until soft, then add the shallots and rosemary, and cook for a further 10 minutes. Add the cider, boil for 10 minutes, then pour on the stock. Simmer until sauce consistency. Pass through a fine sieve, then whisk in a tablespoon of butter. Add the diced apple to the sauce and check for seasoning.

When the sweetbreads are cool enough, gently peel off the outer membrane and any fatty sinew. The sweetbreads will break up into smaller nuggets the size of large plums. Dry them well and roll in the seasoned flour. Shallow fry in the oil and a little butter until golden-brown on all sides. Serve these delicious morsels with a creamy mash or braised endives.

ALAIN CHAPEL'S DUCK TERRINE

MAKES 2 TERRINES
150g duck liver
100g raw foie gras
1 tablespoon duck fat
2 shallots, chopped
1 sprig thyme
1 bay leaf
2 tablespoons brandy
500g duck meat, trimmed of fat and sinew
200g chicken leg meat
200g fatty pork neck meat
350g pork fat
50g foie gras, cooked
50ml double cream
30ml truffle juice
30ml Madeira
salt, pepper freshly ground

First make the 'farce à gratin'. Sear the duck liver and raw foie gras in a very hot frying pan with the duck fat. After a few seconds, add the chopped shallots, thyme and bay, then season well. When the livers are still very pink, add the brandy and take off the heat. Press all this, including the liquid, though a coarse drum sieve, and set aside.

Cut all the other meats and fat into small chunks, season with salt, pepper, cover and refrigerate overnight. Next day, mince using a hand mincer with a 5mm size disc. It is best to refrigerate the mincer before using to keep everything as cold as possible.

Once this is done, add the farce à gratin, foie gras, cream, truffle juice and Madeira. Line a 22 x 18cm terrine with fat or bacon and fill with the mixture. Cook in a bain-marie at 150°C/Gas 2 for about two hours. Leave to cool, then refrigerate overnight. Next day, slice and serve with warm bread and a simple salad.

SABODET À LA LYONNAISE

The sabodet is a coarse pork sausage studded with pieces of snout, ear and jowl of pork. It is a traditional dish of the region and can easily feed four people. If the idea of ears and snout puts you off, use a regular saucisson Lyonnais, studded with pistachios or truffles.

SERVES 4

1 sabodet
6–8 potatoes
4 onions
duck fat or butter
2 cloves garlic, crushed
2 bay leaves
sprig of thyme
salt, pepper
chicken or vegetable stock (see p. 304)

Remove the strings from the sausage. Peel and slice the potatoes. Peel and slice the onions and pan fry them in a little duck fat or butter until golden.

Put the onions into a deep, cast-iron casserole dish with the sausage and potatoes. Add the garlic, bay leaves and thyme, and season well with salt and pepper. Pour onto this just enough chicken or vegetable stock to cover the potatoes and sausage when pressed. Bring to a simmer, then cover and place in oven at 120°C/Gas ½ for 1 hour. Leave to rest out of oven for 30 minutes before taking out and slicing the sausage. Great with a glass of Beaujolais and a bunch of friends.

TARTINE DE GIBIER
GAME TOASTS

SERVES 6–8

6 small birds (thrush, blackbirds, pigeons)
olive oil
3 cloves garlic, peeled
slices of baguette
salt, pepper

Remove the innards from the birds and set the hearts and livers aside. Roast the birds in a hot oven, 200°C/Gas 6, with a little olive oil and the garlic cloves for 25–30 minutes, depending on their size. When cooked, add the liver and hearts to the roasting tin, then leave everything to cool.

Take all the meat off the bones. Using a big knife, chop the meat with the garlic, hearts and livers until almost a paste. Add the roasting fats and juices. Check for seasoning, then spread thickly over lightly toasted slices of baguette bread liberally doused with a good olive oil.

Bake in a hot oven for a few minutes and serve with a bitter leaf salad.

STEAK TARTARE

My preference is to use sirloin or rump steak for a tartare. The beef should be best quality, not frozen, and hung for about a week.

SERVES 2

500g steak, trimmed of sinew and fat
1 tablespoon chopped gherkins
1 tablespoon superfine capers
4 shallots, finely chopped
2 egg yolks
1 tablespoon tomato ketchup
1 tablespoon Worcestershire sauce
1 tablespoon Dijon mustard
2 tablespoons chopped parsley
dash of brandy
salt, pepper and Tabasco to taste

Chop the meat into very small pieces by hand and place in a bowl over ice to keep cool until needed. You can chop the meat two hours ahead but no earlier.

When you're ready to serve, mix in all the remaining ingredients. Serve with chips and salad – nothing else will do.

la cuisine originale de cette carte
et inspirée de Mionnay
Mon équipe de cuisiniers ici, avec à
leur tête Masaru Kamikashimoto
a toute ma confiance
Je vous souhaite un bon appétit
et vous offre pour le début du repas

Petite friture du lac Biwa, persil
à panne de céleris frit

Alain Chapel

このメニューのオリジナル料理は
ミヨネーで生まれたものです。
そして、ここ神戸のスタッフは
上柿元 勝をはじめとして、
全てにおいて私の信頼するところです。
なお、お食事のはじめに
小魚・パセリ・セロリ葉のフライを
ご用意いたします。
どうぞお召しあがりください。

アラン・シャペル

After our lunch at Paul Bocuse my father and mother and I just collapsed on the banks of the Soane river and lay in the afternoon sun. It was an amazing experience. We also went to Pierre Orsi, who had a two-star restaurant and a one-star bistro. We ate in the bistro and had 500 grams of steak tartare, seasoned in front of us and served with big fat chips. And then I had a whole St Marcellin cheese, washed down with copious amounts of Beaujolais.

I couldn't have had a better time or been in a better place for learning about food. Lyon and the region around it has a great culinary history – salads, tripe, pâtés, salamis, sausages, chickens and freshwater fish. And it's right on the doorstep of the Beaujolais, Burgundy and Rhône wine regions.

In my second year with Alain Chapel in Lyon, he said he needed me to fly with him to New York to cook a private dinner for 12 people. My eyes lit up. New York! On Concorde no less! His English was very poor, so it helped that I was completely fluent in English. He gave me the dates and the menu – typical Alain Chapel. The starter was pigeon jelly and crayfish, then chicken cooked in a pig's bladder, followed by five or six different desserts, including walnut tart, oeufs à la neige, pear tart and pistachio ice cream.

We packed up all the food in big polystyrene boxes – we even took our own butter – and left Mionnay for Charles de Gaulle airport. But when we arrived at the check-in counter, they looked at my passport and said, 'You have no visa.' I was travelling with my French passport, and it didn't even cross my mind that I needed a visa. I was practically weeping and M. Chapel had steam coming out of his ears. But he wasn't going to let something like a visa get in his way. He got on the telephone and very quickly, within an hour, he arranged for me to go to Paris for an immediate interview at the American Embassy and hopefully a stamp on my passport.

M. Chapel got on the plane, still steaming, and I arrived at the embassy, jumped the queue and was seen by someone very senior, who had his feet up on the desk and was puffing a big cigar. I explained the situation to him, but he clearly knew more about it than I did. He told me to go to a certain counter and they stamped

Alain Chapel's opening statement on the menu of his restaurant in Tokyo. The restaurant opened in the early '80s, under the direction of head chef Kami Kakimoto.

my passport. I rushed out to the taxi and back to the airport only to find I'd missed the second Concorde flight. So I was put on the next 747 – but first-class. I'd never been in first-class before – champagne, caviar, it was superb. But I missed Concorde.

I had responsibility for all the food so when I arrived in New York I had to collect these big polystyrene boxes from the carousel. It looked very odd and I thought, 'Here we go, back to my mother's days with the English customs officers.' I could see a group of people beyond customs, gesturing me to go to a certain official. As I got to the official, he asked me what was in the boxes and I told him. He looked at me and said, 'You know you're not allowed to do this.' I was in complete despair again. If I couldn't get the food through customs, how were we going to cook this fantastic dinner?

The customs officer opened up one box, and pulled out a carrot, still with the dirt on it because that's the way we received them from the farm. I thought he'd have a fit because Americans are so hygiene conscious and there was all this soil everywhere. I just stood there, terrified that all our precious food was going to be confiscated, but he said, 'Well, these look good,' and motioned me through. Imagine if he'd pulled out a pig's bladder or a poulet de Bresse with its head and feathers still on!

Phew. I was so relieved and walked out. Chapel was there with a big smile on his face. We loaded the food into a huge Cadillac and a chauffeur drove us to our hotel on Central Park. The next morning, we went off with our boxes of food to a huge penthouse just off Fifth Avenue, with an amazing view of Central Park.

We set to work. The kitchen was small but perfectly fine, although I couldn't churn ice cream there. I had to walk down Fifth Avenue in my chef's clothes to the hotel to use their kitchen for that. There I was, clutching all my ingredients, scurrying down one of the smartest streets in the world. The shoppers stared, but I didn't care. I was just anxious to make my ice cream.

The dinner was a birthday surprise for a very wealthy American client. When the man came home, the first person he saw was his butler who wished him good evening, to which the man replied,

'Aren't you going to wish me Happy Birthday?' And then he turned round to see his friends and the great chef himself, and the little commis standing beside him – me! It was an amazing evening and I got to fly back on Concorde.

We also went to Morocco to cook for a member of the Royal Family – M. Chapel, myself and a couple of other staff members. M. Bise, from L'Auberge du Père Bise, had also been invited to cook there and we all met up at the airport in Lyon. M. Bise liked a drink, so he took us off to the bar – we didn't need much prompting. Several rounds later, we realised we were in danger of missing our flight! We just made it and flew off to one of the amazing family palaces in Fez. This was a very different challenge in that we were using locally sourced ingredients. We cooked a mini menu – five starters, five main courses and the full dessert menu – and we did that for a week.

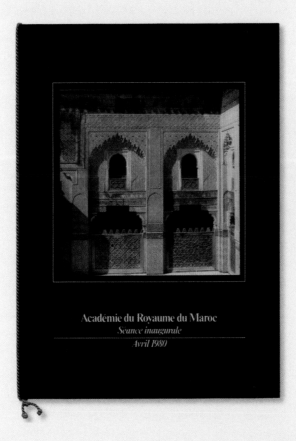

Académie du Royaume du Maroc
Séance inaugurale
Avril 1980

**The menu cover from
our week in Morocco.**

SALADE MAROCAINE

4 red peppers
4 green peppers
4 yellow peppers
2 red onions, peeled and thinly sliced
2 cloves garlic, crushed
juice of 2 lemons
salt, pepper
pinch of ground cumin
pinch of ground coriander
olive oil
coriander leaves

Roast the peppers under a hot grill until they are black all over. Leave to cool, then scrape off the blackened skin. Remove the stems and seeds and cut the peppers into strips.

Add the thinly sliced onion, crushed garlic and some of the lemon juice. Season to taste with salt, pepper, cumin and coriander. Sprinkle with olive oil, the rest of the lemon juice and roughly chopped coriander leaves.

LAMB TAJINE

SERVES 4-6

1 boned lamb shoulder, cut into 3cm chunks
2 tablespoons olive oil
2 cloves garlic, peeled and chopped
3 onions, peeled and chopped
2 teaspoons turmeric
2 teaspoons coriander seeds, crushed
2 teaspoons cumin seeds
1 lemon, cut into 8 wedges
1 tablespoon honey
300ml vegetable or chicken stock (see p. 304)
50g whole blanched almonds, toasted

In a cast-iron casserole, pan fry the lamb in the oil until golden. Over moderate heat, add the garlic, onion and spices to the pan and continue to cook and stir for 10–15 minutes. Then add the lemon, honey and stock.

Bring to a simmer, cover and place in the oven at 140°C/Gas 1 for 1 hour. Then stir in the toasted almonds. Serve in traditional tajine dishes if you have them.

FOUR

Under orders

You can't just get to work in the Elysée Palace with luck. My time there was more than a bit arranged, it was very much arranged. Only by knowing someone and being recommended can you get in there. You have to be in the army and they only took on six conscripts every year. There were 12 in the kitchen altogether, but the other six were permanent army members.

My father knew the head chef at the time, Marcel Le Servot, and Marcel promised he would do his best to get me taken on there. Therefore I agreed to being called up. Obviously I had a choice because I had dual nationality – French and English. I could have renounced my French citizenship and avoided National Service. My original view was that it would be a waste of a year to be called up because I wanted to get on with my career. But this was an opportunity to keep my French citizenship and actually learn something. So my father pulled the strings and made all the phone calls and they accepted me.

First, I had to do two months of basic army training at the barracks at Fontainebleau – learning how to march, how to put a gas mask on, that kind of stuff. I was sleeping in a dorm with 50 others. It was tedious but not entirely unenjoyable. I just got on with it because it was a means to an end. It was hard work and not what I liked doing, but that sort of discipline is good for you really. When you're thrown in with anybody and everybody, you're all in at the same level, which is fantastic. There were kids from the French nobility mixing with young delinquents. You had to get on together some how and work as a team and we all had to be very respectful to our sergeant major.

The food was pretty awful. The standing joke was that when they mowed the lawn in front of the barracks there would be spinach for lunch, and this actually did happen three times during the two months I was at Fontainebleau! There it would be on the table – chopped spinach, this green, grey, brownish muck and you'd think to yourself, 'Can this be true?'

OPPOSITE: Life in the kitchens at the Elysée Palace was hard work – but we had some fun too.

When we went out on bivouac, the rations were pretty abysmal – dried biscuits, some canned corned beef, which they don't call corned beef in France, but *singe* or monkey. Every box of these rations would have a bar of chocolate and a little bottle of really rough eau de vie or brandy, basically firewater.

Then we were given 20 or so blanks to fire and sent on mock missions in nearby woods. Most of the young men charged around taking the whole business very seriously, but I just refused to get involved with this malarkey of pretending to shoot people. I ended up spending the three days hiding in a bush, trading in my blanks with the other soldiers for little bottles of brandy and bars of chocolate. I survived on brandy and chocolate for three days, so my memories of the time are understandably a bit hazy.

One thing I do remember very clearly is worrying about missing my chance to work in the kitchen because there was a general election coming up. If there was a change of government, there might be staff changes as well and that included changes in the palace kitchen. And if my contacts were going to be moved on, perhaps I might miss out.

Fortunately that didn't happen and so I started working in the kitchens just in time for the final weeks of Valéry Giscard D'Estaing's presidency – his final hurrah – and then spent a year working for François Mitterand.

It was a wonderful time. Giscard d'Estaing was leaving so we saw a lot of *au revoir* banquets and parties. He was a great gourmet and very particular. One weekend I was working in the kitchens by myself on a Sunday night – weekends weren't our busiest time so there was a skeleton staff. There were lots of telephones in the kitchen, but only one that connected to the president's suite of rooms. And it rang. The voice on the other end of the phone said, 'I want some oysters, a dozen oysters.' My heart sank because I knew we had no oysters in the fridge. I didn't know what to do. I panicked, but we HAD to get oysters because that's what the President wanted.

The Palace is about a 25-minute walk from the Champs Elysées, but I sprinted down there, still wearing my chef's uniform, to one

Cassolettes de fruits de mer Romanof

Suprêmes de canettes à la Bohèmienne
sur lit de cèpes

Petits pois nouveaux au beurre

Asperges d'Argenteuil

Fromages

Nougatine glacée aux pommes vertes

Domaine de Chevalier 1973

Chapelle Chambertin 1969

Champagne Pommery 1975

Dîner

offert par

Monsieur le Président de la République

et

Madame Valéry Giscard d'Estaing

en l'honneur

des Membres du Secrétariat Général

Lundi 18 Mai 1981

A menu for a ministers' dinner at the Elysée Palace around the time I started work there.

of those seafood brasseries at the bottom of the avenue and came charging back. Giscard d'Estaing had his oysters. I might have been a bit out of breath, but at least the president had his oysters. He was a great gourmet, but what Frenchman isn't?

After the changeover from Giscard d'Estaing to Mitterand, we were scared because the Socialists hadn't been in power for a long time and a lot of the staff worried they'd lose their jobs. They were also very worried about the style of food they were going to be cooking. As in England, where people perceive Labour voters to be keen on pies and chips, the rumours in the kitchen were that with the Socialists we were in for chicken and chips, and not the foie gras and lobster of previous eras.

We were wrong, wrong, wrong. It was absolutely the reverse. The Socialists knew how to party and they certainly did so in great style. It was a fantastic time for me. For the first few months, the government had to thank and entertain a lot of people. So it meant there were banquets, state banquets and dinners. They wanted to show off the best France had to offer, again and again. It was the only time I've seen truffle used as a vegetable and not a garnish.

Edgar Degas (1834-1917)   Musée du Louvre

Résidence de France
Copenhague

Foie gras des Landes truffé

Navarin de homards bretons

Riz sauvage

Fromages de France

Mousse de poire en nougatine

Château Lafaurie-Peyraguey 1975
Corton-Charlemagne (Louis Latour) 1971
Bonnes-Mares (Chanson Père et Fils) 1969
Taittinger Comtes de Champagne 1973

Menu for a state dinner at the Elysée Palace. The covers of state dinner menus always featured something such as a painting from the Louvre or other national archive.

In fact I've never seen so much truffle. And there were lobsters, foie gras, you name it. It was phenomenal.

Those banquets were amazing. As far as the eye could see, there were lobsters dressed on silver platters, all within a millimetre of the same distance to the edge of the plate. I'd learned a lot of precision from my time as a pastry chef, but this was something else altogether. Everything was timed to the second. It was run like a military operation and nothing was left to chance. It was a very well-oiled machine and everyone knew exactly what they were doing. We were serving 200 people at a state banquet and everything had to be done perfectly.

For state dinners, we didn't serve elaborate canapés. I used to do fingers of puff pastry rolled in cheese or poppy seeds and served warm. Or we would serve swarm roasted almonds and hazelnuts. If it was purely a cocktail function, then we would prepare very traditional canapés.

Everything on the menu for state banquets was always served on silver platters and the guests would help themselves. That way they didn't have to have very large portions if they didn't want to. The other thing we learned about silver service for banquets is that you always had to prepare much more food than was actually necessary. Each dish was supposed to serve eight people, but you would put ten portions on the dish so the last person to be served didn't feel they were scraping the dregs off the plate and the first person to be served could see there was plenty of food and didn't have to hold back. There was the odd occasion when one guest would overdo it and the waiters would come rushing down in a panic saying they needed more food, but there was always a contingency plan. We never ran out of anything. The kitchens were much too well organised for that.

The desserts were never plated either. There was always the most wonderful and sumptuous presentation of pastries on silver trays and guests helped themselves. Very often there would be a huge platter of cut fruit put on the table as well. It was very grand, but very private house in style. That's basically what the Elysée Palace was – a very large and very well run private house. It was a style of cooking my father knew very well, from his time in embassies and working with the Cazalet family. It's called *maison bourgeoise* and it's classic food.

The plates and table settings were always arranged by in-house staff. There were staff responsible for the china, and others who looked after the glasses and the cutlery. They all wore gloves to keep things clean and polished, even when just putting them away. Everything was just so pristine.

Almond puff pastry sticks

Roll out pure butter puff pastry to a thickness of about 3mm and brush with beaten egg. Sprinkle generously with nibbed almonds and dust with paprika. Cut into strips 15cm long by 1cm wide.

Take each strip and twirl 5 times before placing it on a baking sheet. Press down the extremities to make sure it holds its shape. Cook in a preheated oven at 200°C/Gas 6 until golden and cooked – 12–15 minutes. These are best eaten when still warm.

Truffles

I love truffles. We get them all year round now. The summer and spring truffles are not as pungent or flavoursome as the autumn ones or the white ones from Alba or Piedmont. But they are all wonderful accompaniments, with each type of truffle having its own particular use.

Truffles really are something special. They are best served with something unctuous like risotto or eggs. The French serve them with foie gras and that works well. Summer truffles are best in thin shavings on something cold. They're not really good to cook, whereas the black truffle can be cooked and put into sauces. The white Alba truffles are always served raw, shaved over a risotto, pasta or egg dishes.

When we're in France, in the truffle season, a man from the village nearby collects and sells truffles and each type has its own particular flavour. The ones with the most intense flavour come from the gravelly ground around vines. He digs them out and you can actually see how the truffle has grown around the vine or the stones themselves. So they have a very odd shape but the most wonderful fragrance and taste. I normally buy them for the restaurant, but my daughter Emily sniffs them out, scrubs them down and uses them on scrambled eggs for breakfast!

You need to take care that your truffles are not overpowered by whatever you serve them with, and that they are not just used as decoration. If you are going to use truffles, be generous with them.

Le Président de la République
et Madame François Mitterrand

prient Monsieur Roux

L'assister à la réception offerte aux collaborateurs de la Présidence,
le jeudi 29 Octobre 1981, à 17 heures 30, au Palais de l'Elysée.
Tenue de ville - Uniforme

Monsieur ROUX

The official invitation for the reception to welcome the incoming president.

For the important banquets at the Elysée Palace, the most ornate china, always in regal blue from Limoges, would come out, together with the gold-plated cutlery. It was counted out and counted in and we were always terrified of handling it in case we dropped something or cracked it. I never got to see the actual stores, because there was a lot of security and everything was locked away very carefully. And we weren't allowed to go upstairs to see the banqueting rooms, although I did know guests sat at long tables, not at a series of round ones.

Guests were served only the finest wines, and they were all French. The wines were chosen by the sommeliers. Even for a casual lunch or dinner, the sommeliers chose the wines with great care. Sadly, I never got to see the cellar, although I knew it was huge. It was kept under lock and key – several locks and keys, in fact.

President Mitterand personally checked and oversaw all the menus for state banquets. There was never any question about this, and he had very definite tastes. The head chef, Marcel Le Servot, would go up to see him with his menus and come back with big red lines all over his pages and comments on certain dishes and about his choice of dinner. You could always tell when the meeting didn't go very well because he'd come charging back down to the kitchens, mumbling and whinging to himself, but making sure everyone could see and hear. Many was the time I saw Marcel coming down in a complete rage, slamming doors and rattling pots and pans because Mitterand had disagreed with his choice of dishes.

Marcel would throw his menus onto his desk. Above his desk was a portrait of the president of the time, and he'd look up, shake his fist and start swearing at it.

Breakfast was served only to President Mitterand and for the last few months of my time there I was in charge of preparing it for him. Like most Frenchmen, he had a gargantuan appetite. He was told by his dietitian that he had to eat a good breakfast, and also a lot of seafood. So sometimes he had oysters, and occasionally he had a mollusc called violet. Or he would ask for scrambled eggs which I would make for him with lashings of butter and cream. Not particularly healthy, but absolutely delicious.

I served the scrambled egg in a big brioche that was about the size of a football. The brioche was cooked fresh every day by the pastry chef. I would scoop out the centre and fill it with scrambled egg and Mitterand would just help himself. He could just take a

---

Perfect creamy scrambled eggs
SERVES 4

8 free-range eggs
2 tablespoons unsalted butter
4 tablespoons double cream
salt, freshly ground pepper

Take a heavy saucepan and smear the butter inside. Break the eggs into the pan. Place over a medium to high heat and, using a wooden spatula, start to break up the eggs and stir. (Never, ever use a whisk). With the spatula, scrape the pan to lift off the egg that is catching on the base. Continue to cook and gently stir – do not beat. The eggs should have big chunks of white and yolk clearly defined. When the eggs are almost completely cooked, yet still a little runny, take off the heat and add the cream, salt and pepper. Leave for 2–3 minutes in a warm place before serving.

slice of the brioche with the egg. There would be Parma ham on the side, or sometimes sea urchins on the top. He never ate the whole thing, so we had the leftovers to finish off back in the kitchen – completely delicious.

After two or three months of eating like this, the dietitian decided Mitterand's health wasn't improving. He had to go on a diet. So some of the banquets took a different direction. And that's when Marcel got really upset – having to use reduced-fat butter and cream, and redesign the menus.

Our work down in the palace kitchens wasn't all banquets and state dinners. We also had to feed the staff, the secretaries and any of the MPs who were in the palace at the time. And everything had to be perfect. The blanquette de veau, the navarin of lamb, the vegetables – everything had to be the best. Even if there were chips, they had to be hand cut. It wasn't just staff food; it was for MPs and their aides, and occasionally the President would eat from the lunch menu too.

Each morning we were told how many people would be requiring lunch. Most days it was 40 to 50 people but perhaps only ten on the weekends. We were split up into groups under the guidance of one of the full-time chefs. The leader of my group, Bernard, is now actually head chef! Another of the conscripts was Christian Têtedoie, who's running a one-star restaurant in Lyon, and David Martin, son of Jacques Martin, the famous French comedian and television presenter, who died recently.

At the Palace, we cooked very classic food. For me, it was another learning curve – how to cook all those classic dishes. We cooked all the classic starters as well – proper beetroot salad, proper potato salad, crudités, red cabbage salad, which was marinated overnight. It was very French, very straightforward and very classical. One particular dish I remember was a *macreuse*, a cut of beef very similar to silverside. The whole joint was larded with pork, roasted, and then braised, covered in stock and wine. Then it was slow cooked for the best part of seven or eight hours and served either hot or cold. It would completely melt in the mouth.

BEETROOT SALAD

The best beetroots for salad are a long variety called Crapaudine.
For all recipes, beetroot is always better roasted rather than boiled.

SERVES 4

500g beetroot
coarse salt
red wine vinegar
olive oil
salt
olive oil
salt, pepper
Brittany shallots, peeled and thinly sliced
parsley, chopped

Wash and scrub the beetroots if necessary. Place in a pan on a bed of coarse salt and bake in an hot oven, 180°C/Gas 4, for an hour, depending on size. The beetroot should be tender when pierced with a knife. When cool enough to handle, peel away the skin and cut up the flesh into dice.

Season while still warm with a generous splash of red wine vinegar, olive oil, salt and pepper. Add the shallots and chopped parsley.

RED CABBAGE SALAD

SERVES 8-10

120ml red wine vinegar
1 clove
3 blades of mace
sea salt and black pepper
1 red cabbage
vegetable oil (not olive oil)
coarse grain mustard

Bring the red wine vinegar to the boil and add the clove and mace.

Take a firm red cabbage and cut into quarters. Remove the outer leaf and core. Slice the cabbage very thinly and place in a large earthenware or stainless steel bowl. Season with a little sea salt and pepper. Remove the spices from the hot vinegar and pour it onto the cabbage. Cover the bowl. Every 10–15 minutes, toss the cabbage around so it soaks up the seasoning. Do this 4 or 5 times, then leave overnight.

The following day, drizzle with a neutral vegetable oil (olive oil does not work well with cabbage) and a little mustard.

POTATO SALAD

SERVES 4–6

400g waxy potatoes
4 spring onions, trimmed and sliced
8 tablespoons olive oil
1 tablespoon Dijon mustard
2 tablespoons white wine vinegar
salt, pepper

To make the best potato salad you need a good waxy potato and it must be cooked with the skin. Once the potatoes are cooked, remove the skin and cut into thick slices. Season with sliced spring onions and a vinaigrette made with olive oil, Dijon mustard and white wine vinegar. Pour this over the potatoes while they are still warm and they will soak up some of the dressing.

Another favourite Roux variation is to season the potatoes with a generous spoon of crème fraîche and mayonnaise – indulgent, rich and delicious served with smoked fish.

We'd even do things like hachis parmentier – shepherd's pie – at the Elysée Palace, but to perfection. And we used to do a dish I thought was a bit peculiar at the time, but it tastes incredibly good. Oeufs à la tripe – eggs in tripe fashion – is made with hard-boiled eggs, but again Marcel was very particular about the boiled eggs. If you overcook a hard-boiled egg, you get that horrible green edge to the yolk and they smell horrible. Marcel would check every single egg to make sure it was not overdone.

We never put eggs into boiling water, never. You put the eggs into cold water and time them from when the water reaches boiling point – 90 seconds for soft-boiled and six minutes for hard. That way you get a better result and the shells never crack. The egg is more evenly cooked as well.

Anyway, we would hard-boil the eggs and then fry off some white onions so they were cooked well but not coloured. They still had to have a bit of hold to them. Then we would sprinkle them all over the eggs, make a béchamel sauce with plenty of nutmeg and white pepper, pour it over the onion and eggs, grate some cheese on top and put it in the oven. The MPs loved it and so did the staff. It's a simple classic dish and it doesn't have to be heavy or gluggy if it is well cooked. And it's cheap too.

We made the blanquette de veau from the belly and ribs of the veal calf. We always had to have a bit of bone in there as well. Basically it's simmered until soft and then the cooking liquid is reduced and then thickened again with a roux. Finally it's finished with a bit of crème fraîche and an egg yolk. The meat is then returned to the sauce and served with onions and various other vegetables and a rice pilaf. It's as traditional as navarin of lamb or boeuf bourgignon, which we also served often. We cooked a lot of whole trout, whiting, mackerel and coalfish, too.

During my first winter at the Elysée Palace, I was asked to cook for some of the presidential shooting weekends. The President had two châteaux just outside Paris, in Rambouillet and Marly, where he and his guests shot pheasants, wild duck and partridge. Both were typical French châteaux with turrets. They were beautiful. The chef

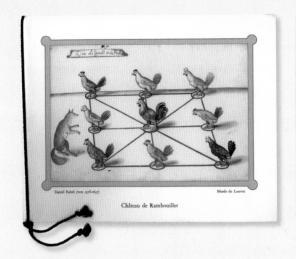

Quiche aux St-Jacques
Suprêmes de faisane à la Bohémienne
Pommes moulées Forestière
Fromages
Soufflé glacé aux marrons

Rayne Sec 1979
Beaune 1971

Château de Rambouillet.

Menu for a shooting party at the Château de Rambouillet.

had asked for volunteers to cook there and I was straight in for that. It was a new experience and there was a bonus payment as well. After I had helped on a few weekends, the head chef decided I was capable of doing it on my own, so I was driven down with all the food and another conscript on the Friday.

The first job we had to do was to stoke up the stove, a huge, ancient, coal-fired oven. There was quite a knack to getting this going and it took all Friday night and a fair number of anxious moments to get it hot enough so that on Saturday we could cook breakfast for the presidential party. We used to do a picnic lunch for them – invariably something hot like a soup or a rich stew. Saturday night would be a proper sit-down dinner, always based around game. Of course, by the time we left on Sunday the stove would be glowing. We'd damp it down and drive back to Paris with our free brace of pheasant.

In my two years at the Elysée Palace, there was nothing modern about the food we cooked there, no nouvelle cuisine. It was all done in the old traditional way, which was fantastic because it meant I was seeing something else as well as learning an immense amount.

People always think a chef does nothing but cook, but in reality there's a huge amount of cleaning to do as well. At the Elysée Palace, we did all the cleaning ourselves. The kitchen was huge, with a labyrinth of corridors leading off to different rooms.

HACHIS PARMENTIER
SHEPHERD'S PIE

For me, the best shepherd's pie is made with leftover roast lamb, either shoulder or leg. In fact, I remember my sister and myself holding back on a Sunday lunch in case there wasn't enough left to make the pie. When we roast meat in the Roux household we always add some vegetables, such as carrot, onion and celery, to the roasting tin. These are vital for the making of a good moist pie.

leftover roast lamb and vegetables
tomato ketchup
Worcestershire sauce
1 clove garlic
mashed potato (see p.159)
butter

Scrape off all the meat and fat off the bone and add any scraps that are left. Add the vegetables and roasting juices, then put everything through a mincing machine. Mix in a spoonful of tomato ketchup and a splash of Worcestershire sauce. Rub the pie dish with a cut clove of garlic, then spread the meat evenly in the dish.

Top with smooth mashed potato and dot with a few pieces of butter. Bake until golden and piping hot.

ROAST PIGEON WITH CHARTREUSE

Squab pigeons reared for the table are delicious. They taste rich
and gamey but not as strong, or chewy, as woodpigeon.

SERVES 4

4 squab pigeons, about 350g each
2 tablespoons olive oil
2 tablespoons butter
salt, pepper
3 shallots, finely chopped
1 large carrot, peeled and finely chopped
2 sticks celery, peeled and finely chopped
2 tablespoons green Chartreuse
250ml brown chicken stock (see p. 305)
1 tablespoon chopped thyme leaves
knob of butter

Put the pigeons in a roasting tin or cast-iron cocotte with the oil and
a tablespoon of the butter. Season well and roast for about 20 minutes
at 200°C/Gas 6 for pink meat. Take the pigeons out of the oven and
leave to rest in a warm place. Drain and discard the fat from the pan.

Put the roasting pan back on the stove with the rest of the butter and
sweat the shallot, carrot and celery. Once the vegetables are tender
but not coloured, add the Chartreuse. Reduce by half, then pour in
the brown chicken stock. Boil and reduce until sauce consistency.
Finish with a few thyme leaves and a knob of butter to shine and
enrich the sauce.

OEUFS À LA TRIPE
EGGS IN TRIPE FASHION

SERVES 4

3 onions
olive oil
1 tablespoon butter
1 heaped tablespoon plain flour
500ml milk
salt, pepper, nutmeg
4 eggs, hard-boiled
100g Gruyère or Emmental cheese, grated

Peel the onions, cut them in half and slice. Cook in a little olive oil until lightly browned and tender, then drain on kitchen paper. Make a roux with the butter and flour. Add the milk, whisk well and cook to make a white sauce. Season well with salt, pepper and nutmeg.

Preheat the oven to 180°C/Gas 4. Cut the eggs in half and place them yolk-side down in a buttered, ovenproof dish. Scatter the onions onto the eggs and then pour over the sauce. Sprinkle the cheese on top and bake in the oven until hot and golden brown – this should take 10–15 minutes. Finish browning the top under the grill if necessary.

VEAL BLANQUETTE

SERVES 6-8

1kg breast of veal, cut into
    4 cm chunks
1 large onion, studded with
    2 cloves
2 carrots, peeled
1 leek, white part only
1 bouquet garni
salt

GARNISH

24 small cocktail onions, peeled
250g small button mushrooms

SAUCE

300ml double cream
2 egg yolks whisked with 2
    tablespoons crème fraîche
salt, pepper

Put the meat in a pan, cover generously with cold water and bring to the boil. Turn down to a gentle simmer and skim off any froth. After 30 minutes, add the vegetables, bouquet garni and a little salt. Continue to simmer for a further 80 minutes – you may need to top up with boiling water.

While this meat is simmering, carefully decant about half a litre of the cooking liquid and pour over the small cocktail onions in a separate pan. Simmer until tender, then add the trimmed mushrooms. Cover and simmer for a further 10 minutes until cooked. Now drain and pour the liquid back into the meat pot. Keep the garnish warm in a tureen. When the meat is tender, gently drain off and put in the tureen, discarding the vegetables. Cover and keep warm.

Bring the cooking liquid to a rapid boil for 15 minutes or until reduced by half. Add the double cream, boil again for 5 minutes, then off the heat stir in the whisked egg yolk mixture. Check for seasoning and pour though a fine sieve over the meat and garnish.

WILD DUCK WITH GIROLLE MUSHROOMS

SERVES 2

1 wild mallard duck
80g smoked duck breast
160g girolle mushrooms, cleaned
2 shallots, peeled and chopped
1 tablespoon vegetable oil
1 tablespoon brandy
2 tablespoons Madeira
1 tablespoon chopped flat-leaf parsley
2 dessertspoons butter
salt, pepper

Trim and prepare the duck for roasting. Trim some of the fat off the smoked duck and cut into medium dice. Cut up the mushrooms if necessary. Take a cast-iron pan, small enough for the bird to fit snugly, and heat up the oil until smoking. Place the seasoned duck in the pan and sear on all sides. Put in the oven at 200°C/Gas 6 for 10 minutes. Then add 1 spoonful of butter and continue to cook for a further 10 minutes, turning and basting twice. Remove the duck and leave in a warm place to rest. Discard most of the fat, leaving a little for cooking the shallots.

In the same pan, cook the shallots over a moderate heat for a few seconds. Add the mushrooms and continue to cook until they are soft and have rendered some of their water. Pour in the brandy and Madeira, bring to the boil and fold in the rest of the butter, the smoked duck and the parsley. Serve the sauce hot with the roasted duck.

The ovens in the Elysée kitchens were huge, too. One of them was so enormous you could cook a side of beef in it. You could fit in three human bodies. I know, because we hid in it one day as a joke – with the oven switched off, of course.

In the middle of the kitchen was a huge marble-topped table that we used for making pastry and where we would sit to eat lunch as well. To one side there was a pot-washing sink so big that it was like a mini-swimming pool or a bath. It was very old fashioned and lined with copper, and there were gas burners underneath to heat up the water. You never told anyone when your birthday came around because invariably you would end up in the full sink – and then have to buy everyone a round of drinks.

Some of the pots and pans dated back to the 1400s. They were made of thick copper and you needed two people to pick them up – and that was when they were empty. They weren't very practical, but they were beautiful. They had to be polished once a week along with all the other copper pans and moulds. We made a paste of

To clean copper

Mix egg white, flour, salt and cheap vinegar together. Rub the paste onto the pans and then wash it off. Take care to dry the copper quickly and thoroughly, otherwise marks will remain.

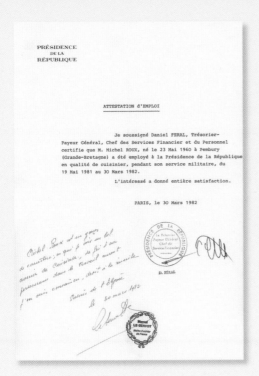

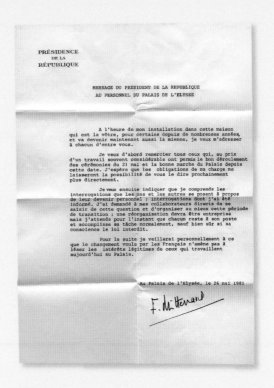

TOP LEFT: My reference from the Elysée Palace – glowing as you would expect!

TOP RIGHT: A letter from President Mitterand, thanking the staff for their hard work and mentioning that if anyone's conscience was troubling them, they could leave.

vinegar, egg white, salt and flour, and then rinsed it off. You had to be very careful to dry it off quickly, otherwise it would spot and you would have to start it all again. We used sandpaper to clean the stoves and with the sandpaper we used to make patterns and decorations. There were little competitions between each team to see who could make the best design.

It was a great time and we also had certain perks. We didn't have to wear uniform and we didn't have to live in the barracks – I got myself a studio nearby. We got two free cartons of cigarettes a month which at the time were handy, and we were paid a bit extra. It was invaluable experience, and even though I thought I might not see the other chefs again, our paths did cross over the years.

Although my grandmother Liliane was in Paris, and my aunt Danielle and Uncle Jean as well, I was pleased to get back home to London. While I was away working in France, Le Gavroche had moved from Lower Sloane Street to Upper Brook Street and won a third Michelin star. More than anything, I wanted to start working with my father and uncle again.

FIVE

The family business

When I came back to London, I began to find my feet as a chef and manager in the family businesses – Gavvers, Le Gamin, Le Poulbot and Le Gavroche, and in contract and private catering. As usual, the hours were long. My family also had a charcuterie, Le Cochon Rose in Sloane Street, but unfortunately that didn't last very long.

Gavvers was in the old Le Gavroche premises in Lower Sloane Street. It was turned into a restaurant serving very simple but good food, things like bouillabaisse, cassoulet, choucroute – hearty provincial dishes. It could seat about 60 and it was very successful. I worked in the kitchens there, but not for that long because then I went to work at Le Gamin, a big brasserie in the Old Bailey. That was busy – 120 seats – and it was a huge place with a big kitchen. We used to run the outside catering from there as well. We did boardroom lunches, private dinners and functions, serving anything from six to 600. It was a massive operation. For boardroom lunches, we'd make dishes such as stews and casseroles that could be cooked ahead of time and kept warm. Every main course had to have a sauce. The food was taken to the boardroom, reheated and then served. It wasn't fabulous, but it was the best that was on offer at the time. It was good fresh food, but there were limitations to what we could do. Sometimes we'd be organising three-day events, every meal to be cooked on site and served in marquees.

It was hectic – sometimes things would go wrong. Once we were catering a massive function at Syon House and of course we set off with masses of time to spare. But the van got a puncture on the way and we couldn't get the tyre off. We had to call the AA and by the time we got back on the road and arrived at Syon House, with all the food still in the back of the van, the guests were already walking in. And this was in the days before mobile telephones. But it was OK in the end, despite the panic.

When I was working on the catering side, Le Gavroche organised an enormous charity dinner, The Birthright Ball at the Royal Albert

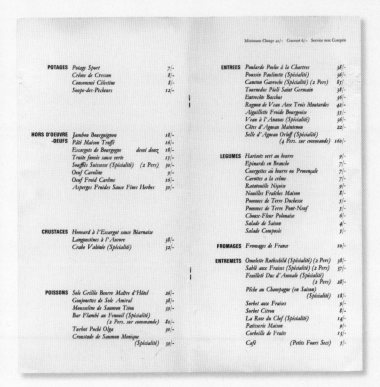

Minimum Charge 40/-   Couvert 6/-   Service non Compris

POTAGES
- Potage Sport — 7/-
- Crème de Cresson — 8/-
- Consommé Célestine — 8/-
- Soupe-des-Pêcheurs — 12/-

HORS D'OEUVRE -OEUFS
- Jambon Bourguignon — 18/-
- Pâté Maison Truffé — 16/-
- Escargots de Bourgogne — demi douz — 18/-
- Truite fumée sauce verte — 15/-
- Soufflés Suissesse (Spécialité) (2 Pers) — 30/-
- Oeuf Caroline — 16/-
- Oeuf Froid Carême — 16/-
- Asperges Froides Sauce Fines Herbes — 30/-

CRUSTACES
- Homard à l'Escargot sauce Béarnaise
- Langoustines à l'Aurore — 38/-
- Crabe Vabinée (Spécialité) — 32/-

POISSONS
- Sole Grillée Beurre Maître d'Hôtel — 26/-
- Goujonettes de Sole Amiral — 38/-
- Mousseline de Saumon Titou — 30/-
- Bar Flambé au Fenouil (Spécialité) (2 Pers. sur commande) — 80/-
- Turbot Poché Olga — 30/-
- Cronstade de Saumon Monique (Spécialité) — 39/-

ENTREES
- Poularde Poelée à la Chartres — 38/-
- Poussin Paulinette (Spécialité) — 36/-
- Caneton Gavroche (Spécialité) (2 Pers) — 85/-
- Tournedos Poêlé Saint Germain — 38/-
- Entrecôte Bacchus — 36/-
- Rognon de Veau Aux Trois Moutardes — 42/-
- Aiguillette Froide Bourgeoise — 35/-
- Veau à l'Ananas (Spécialité) — 36/-
- Côtes d'Agneau Maintenon — 22/-
- Selle d'Agneau Orloff (Spécialité) (4 Pers. sur commande) — 160/-

LEGUMES
- Haricots vert au beurre — 9/-
- Epinards en Branche — 7/-
- Courgettes au beurre ou Provençale — 7/-
- Carottes à la crème — 7/-
- Ratatouille Niçoise — 9/-
- Nouilles Fraîches Maison — 8/-
- Pommes de Terre Duchesse — 5/-
- Pommes de Terre Pont-Neuf — 5/-
- Choux-Fleur Polonaise — 6/-
- Salade de Saison — 4/-
- Salade Composée — 5/-

FROMAGES
- Fromages de France — 10/-

ENTREMETS
- Omelette Rothschild (Spécialité) (2 Pers) — 38/-
- Sablé aux Fraises (Spécialité) (2 Pers) — 37/-
- Feuilleté Duc d'Aumale (Spécialité) (2 Pers) — 28/-
- Pêche au Champagne (en Saison) (Spécialité) — 18/-
- Sorbet aux Fraises — 9/-
- Sorbet Citron — 8/-
- La Rose du Chef (Spécialité) — 14/-
- Pâtisserie Maison — 9/-
- Corbeille de Fruits — 13/-
- Café (Petits Fours Secs) — 5/-

Menu from Le Gavroche in the Lower Sloane Street days.

Hall in London. On the menu was one of my father's signature dishes – oeuf pôché Albert, which was a poached egg in an artichoke heart with smoked salmon. You can imagine trying to poach 2,800 eggs and turning the artichokes, making each one perfect. The main course was a slow-cooked rump of beef, served cold in its own jelly with tiny baby vegetables. The dessert was a tarte citron with a cassis mousse. The work involved in that dinner was phenomenal, and Roux being Roux the majority of it had to be done, not to order, but as close to possible to the time of serving. All the eggs were poached and trimmed in the morning. Each one had to be cooked, then put into iced water to stop it setting, then trimmed up to make a perfect round.

I thought it was going to be a doddle, but it took me about five hours to poach all those eggs. The lemon tarts were made throughout the night before so they were fresh. At that time, my father was pioneering the vacuum-packed way of preserving food. He was looking at ways of cooking and preserving meat, both for restaurants and also for schools and institutions. This was in the early 1980s so he was very ahead of his time. We cooked the beef and sterilised it in the vacuum-packed pouches, so we could actually start the preparation about four weeks beforehand. The restaurant used to be shut then on weekends, so we came in and worked through Saturdays and Sundays before the charity dinner, preparing all the beef.

Every five days we took samples from the packs of meat and had them analysed to make sure the food was all safe. It was very high risk, because if it wasn't still good we would have to do it all again. But it did work and it tasted fantastic.

It was very much a learning curve, particularly when it came to plating the food up and sending it off to the various parts of the Albert Hall, which is a cavernous place. We had managers with walkie-talkies – it was a complete military exercise. I was very glad when it was over.

Catering was hard work. At the end of the evening, you have to dismantle everything, put it in the van, drive back to base and then unload it all again. It was common not to get back before three in the morning. Some clients didn't realise how much effort went into these events and how much hard work, so they often bickered about the price. They couldn't understand why we couldn't cook such and such a dish in the middle of a field in the depths of winter.

But again I learned a lot about speaking to clients and going through menus. I learned about what makes a good menu. It has to be appropriate and it has to make money. It's a common trap for chefs – cooking for guidebooks and cooking for journalists as opposed to cooking for clients and your own business. Because if you don't make money you'll end up with nowhere to cook. A good menu gives clients what they want and it has to be something that you can cook successfully. It has to be practical and suit the surroundings. There's no point in putting a soufflé on a menu if you know you won't be able to cook it properly. You've got to play safe if you want good results.

The Gavvers and Le Gamin period of my career was very much about putting everything I'd learned so far in my jobs and apprenticeships into practice and finding my feet as a manager. I was lucky to be working with my family, but at that time I had no aspirations to take over Le Gavroche. I saw my future as going off and starting my own place, or maybe staying with the brasserie style. I enjoyed that type of food and Le Gamin had a very good reputation.

The outside catering was a thriving business. Also, it changed hugely over the years. Rather than delivering food which needed to be just reheated and served, we were moving into contract catering, which was relatively new then – this meant putting a fully-fledged chef and team into a kitchen at the company and cooking the food there. Getting that up and running took a lot of time but it was the way forward. Our contracts included Grievson and Grant, which merged with Kleinwort Benson, Banque Paribas, Credit Suisse and Merrill Lynch. We still have most of these clients through our consultancy with Compass.

Sauté potatoes

Wash the potatoes – Amandine, Belle de Fontenay or Rooster are ideal – and boil them in their skins. Peel them when they're cool enough to handle. Then cut the potatoes into slices about 5mm thick and pan fry in oil until golden. Season and sprinkle with chopped garlic and parsley.

For even more delicious results, fry the potatoes in some duck fat.

Mashed potato

To make the perfect mash, first choose the right potato. The red skinned Rooster has the texture and flavour to make the tastiest and creamiest of mash. Gently boil the potatoes in their skins in lightly salted water until tender. Peel and press through a ricer or drum sieve, then beat in butter or olive oil, warm milk or for really extravagant mash – double cream. The mash can be kept warm in a bain-marie (water bath) for a couple of hours. To avoid getting a skin on the potato, pour a little warm milk and a few dots of butter on the top.

Composing a menu

When you're having people round for a meal what you don't want to do is to spend all evening in the kitchen, so that means cooking ahead. Get everything you can ready beforehand. Serve a cold starter, something that can be prepared, even plated up ahead of time and only needs a bit of dressing just before people sit down. And make the dressing beforehand. Don't experiment – serve something you know works. Keep it cold and serve some warm bread. That always works beautifully. Or have lots of nibbles with drinks instead of a first course. Home-made sausage rolls can be made the day before and reheated, for example. Go retro. Serve celery sticks with a dip, but a great dip like goat cheese and chives.

For the main course, again go for the tried and tested. If you're having a roast, let it rest for an hour, which means it can be out of the oven before guests are due. Don't try to cook it after they've arrived. Then just before serving, put the meat back into a hot oven for ten minutes and carve it at the table.

A stew is another good idea. Make it the day before, which always tastes better. Serve the stew with a big tray of roasted vegetables which pretty much look after themselves. Or blanch vegetables the day before and then put them back into boiling water for a couple of minutes until they're warm again.

Pudding? Again, the simpler the better. If you've made a cook-ahead main course, such as a stew, you may feel able to tackle a pudding that requires some last-minute attention. Or if the main course is more challenging, stick to a dessert that you can prepare earlier and just plate up at the last minute. Emily's warm, runny chocolate puds (see p. 217) are among our family favourites, and these can be prepared and put in the fridge, ready to be popped into the oven when you're ready – easy and delicious. Seasonal fruits are always popular and nothing could be nicer than a bowl of berries with perhaps some cream, or even home-made ice cream.

BLANQUETTE D'AGNEAU À LA MENTHE
CREAMY LAMB STEW WITH MINT

SERVES 6

4kg shoulder or middle neck of lamb,
   cut into 2cm cubes
1 onion, peeled
2 carrots, peeled
1 leek, cut in half and tied
1 head of garlic, cut in half
1 bouquet garni with mint stalks
2 litres white chicken stock (see p. 304)
250ml white wine
coarse salt
750ml double cream
4 tablespoons shredded mint
juice of 1 lemon

Place the lamb in a pan, cover with cold water and bring to the boil. Cook for 3 minutes and then refresh under cold, running water. Put the lamb in a clean, ovenproof pot with the vegetables and herbs. Cover with stock and wine, bring to the boil and season very lightly with coarse salt. Cover the pot, place in a slow oven, 130°C/Gas 1, and cook for 1¼ hours to 1½ hours until the lamb is soft and tender.

Remove the meat and keep warm. Strain the liquid, then reduce by three-quarters. Add the cream and reduce again by half. Correct the seasoning, then put the meat back into the sauce with the mint and a little lemon juice. Serve with a rice pilaf and a garnish of button onions and mushrooms.

ALMOND AND ORANGE CAKE
WITH WHISKY-SOAKED SEGMENTS

SERVES 8–10

50g plain flour
1 teaspoon baking powder
225g caster sugar
250g ground almonds
250g unsalted butter, room temperature
1 tablespoon grated zest of orange
4 free-range eggs
80ml freshly squeezed orange juice
60g brown sugar
1 tablespoon marmalade
handful of sliced almonds, toasted

Butter a round cake tin, approximately 20cm wide. Preheat the oven to 180°C/Gas 4.

Sift the flour, baking powder and sugar, and add the ground almonds. Whisk the butter with the orange zest until pale, then add the eggs one at a time. Fold in the dry ingredients with a metal spoon. Pour the mixture into the cake tin and bake in the preheated oven for 45 minutes or until cooked.

Meanwhile make a syrup by boiling the orange juice with the brown sugar. Leave to cool. Once the cake is cooked, prick several times with a skewer to the base and pour on the cooled syrup. Leave the cake to cool completely before brushing on a little warmed marmalade and sprinkling it with a few toasted, sliced almonds.

Lovely served with orange segments marinated in a generous splash of whisky and a little demerara sugar.

And we still did some cooking at private houses. Often I'd be called on to cook for six to eight people at the client's home. Many were good customers of Le Gavroche. I would get in the car with the food and a waiter, and off we'd go. They wanted the best food because they were Le Gavroche regulars.

Sometimes it was hard cooking in other people's kitchens, but we just got on with it. I'm never shocked at the state of anyone else's kitchen now. I've seen them all. In the face of adversity you just have to cope – ad lib where necessary and know that with all your past experience you will do it right on the night. I've never had any disasters as far as the clients could see. There may have been disasters in my eyes, times when I've had to cut corners, but you try not to let the client realise this. I enjoyed doing those dinners. It was personal cooking and it was fun and very rewarding.

We used to cook for Andrew Grima, the famous jewellery designer. At one of his dinners I was going to serve a warm lobster salad. I asked if it was all right to heat some pretty glass plates I'd found in the kitchen. He said I could – but one of them just shattered. I carried on cooking and later, as I was leaving, I told him I'd broken a plate and that I would replace it. The next day, I rang his office and they told me it was a Lalique plate! I nearly died, because it was worth probably £1,000 in today's terms.

We don't do much of that any more. There might still be five or six clients we cook for privately at home. I send my head chef or sous-chef and they enjoy it as well. It's important for a chef because it can be the first time you meet a client and it's a big learning curve. Too often chefs are stuck in the kitchen and don't get to meet the people they're cooking for. It's very important to see your clients and I go out into the restaurant every day. It's not easy for me, because I'm shy by nature, but you have to make that effort.

There aren't too many businesses where a 14- to 16-hour day is normal, but that's how it is in restaurants. When people work those kind of hours on a regular basis, they tend to go a bit wild when they finally finish for the day or night. Also, what we're doing is producing the best food we can in an atmosphere where people can enjoy themselves. And that is always conducive to people loosening up and perhaps doing things they wouldn't normally do, both in the kitchen and in front of house.

There is always huge tension in a Michelin-starred kitchen. Because of that, or perhaps because of the pressure and the energy you need, the amount of sexual innuendo that goes on in this business is unbelievable – and the amount of sexual activity. Life in the kitchen is steamy and passionate, very sensual. It's about food and wine and giving. You do give 100 percent to your work, just as you do to a relationship. The sexuality is always there and there's always lots of banter and affairs.

I've seen this in the kitchen ever since my days as an apprentice, from the very petty, childlike games with a carrot to the constant jokes about sex. It's always been a part of the industry and I don't know any other industry like it.

There is not a moment ever goes by in the kitchen without someone talking about sex or generally being crude and I don't know quite why it is. Certainly when I first started as an apprentice, there were no girls and the atmosphere was very much like a locker room – a bunch of guys together. At Alain Chapel there was one girl in the kitchen and that was almost unheard of in those days. She only stayed a month before she moved on. At La Tante Claire there were no females. At Le Gavroche there were a few because my father always insisted on having women in the kitchen. He's always said there is no reason why the girls should not be allowed in the kitchen and that they are as good as the guys – a view that I share. Everyone is treated the same here. Obviously if a girl is small and needs help picking up a pot or lifting something, she'll be helped, but there is no special treatment. If she makes a mistake, a girl will get the same bollocking as a guy.

Still, it's a very male-dominated industry. Kitchens do tame down when there are more women on the staff, although some girls can dish it out as much as the guys. Some can be pretty raucous. There are always lots of affairs in the kitchen, I suppose because everyone is working incredibly long hours and the staff tends to socialise together as well as work together. You get situations where there may be only two or three girls in a team and those girls seem to be shared around. It may not be nice but it happens. In many ways it's quite primitive. It's hard to describe, but it's something I've always been aware of and indeed taken part in. It's just the way it is and it is extremely odd for people who are not used to it.

I remember once in the 1990s we had a young American chef who started at Le Gavroche. We arranged his work permit, his visa, everything. We spent a lot of time and money to bring him over here and after two days he came into my office and said, 'Chef, I'm quitting.' I said, 'Hang on a minute, you've come from the other side of the world. It's your dream to work at Le Gavroche and after two days you're going to throw it in and quit?' And he replied, 'I cannot believe how much swearing goes on in this kitchen and the way you treat the women here.'

I said, 'OK, yes, I swear, but it's not gratuitous. And yes, the girls get the same treatment as the guys. That's the way it is.' He couldn't handle it and so he quit. I was gobsmacked. But I've never had females come up to me and say they're leaving because of the bad language or because they are discriminated against.

I could get very crude with all the stories of sex and kitchen affairs. There is probably not a corner of this place that hasn't seen any action. It is an industry where sex is rampant, not just in the kitchen, but also in the front of house. There are a lot of pent-up feelings and tensions in a restaurant, and there has to be an outlet somewhere. And for much of the time, that outlet is sex.

Perhaps it's the alcohol or the atmosphere, but some of the women guests are very attracted to the staff. And a lot of the waiters have ended up with telephone numbers slipped into their hands at the end of service. There have been many steamy letters written to members of staff, too – very explicit in what the writers would like to do and have done to them.

At Le Gavroche we often have tables of women dining together and then telephone numbers pass hands. And, of course, there have been times when a man has been dining with a woman – and his

OPPOSITE: My early days in the kitchen at Le Gavroche.

wife has walked in with someone else. Or vice versa. Then Silvano, our manager, has to quickly take control and very discreetly say to the guest at the door, 'I'm sorry, but your wife is here tonight,' and then they can quickly leave. There was a time when a man used to bring his mistress here regularly, and his wife used to entertain her lover so the two sometimes clashed appointments. You have to be careful and diplomatic and realise immediately what the situation is. Silvano has always been amazing like that. And we do have a downstairs exit, although it's never had to be used... yet.

Then there is the underwear that's left behind. We've got a special box we keep it in. But funnily enough no one has ever come to claim any of it. We've had couples disappear into the toilets, and not just heterosexual couples. Once two men went into the toilets. One of them was married and his wife was still at the table. And the men took some time to re-appear.

On at least two occasions, underwear has been handed to a waiter in the middle of service. If that's not a way of saying come and get me, I don't know what is. So the waiter has to serve the table for the rest of the night, knowing the woman has no knickers on. I don't know of any marriages which have come out of all this, but certainly there've been relationships that have gone on for some time. Of course, Le Gavroche policy strictly frowns on this, but what happens out of hours – well, you have no control over that. A few years ago, one customer offered to pay one of the commis waiters if he would sleep with his wife!

Perhaps it's down to a combination of things – power, money, the sensuality of good food and wine and the ambience of the restaurant which I've always thought is incredibly comfortable and seductive. And obviously some people get carried away.

BRAISED RUMP POINTS

This is a dish you need to start preparing the day before,
so a good choice when entertaining.

SERVES 4

2 beef rump points
  (about 2kg total weight)
6 strips of pork larding fat
  (16cm long)
1 bottle strong red wine
½ bottle port
1 carrot
1 onion

1 stick celery
olive oil
1 bay leaf
1 shot brandy
salt, pepper
1.5 litres veal stock
  (see p.303)
2 tablespoons butter

Make sure the rump points still have the fat on the side. Using a
larding needle, thread the pork fat evenly though the meat going
with the grain. Put the wine and port in a pan and boil until
reduced by two-thirds. Peel and chop the vegetables.

Heat a little olive oil in a cast-iron pan and sear the seasoned meat
on all sides. Remove the meat and brown the vegetables in the same
pan. Return the meat to the pan with the bay leaf and deglaze with
the brandy. Pour onto this the wine and stock and bring to a simmer.
Skim, then cover and place in the oven at 120°C/Gas ½ for at least 5
hours or until tender. Leave to cool completely and then refrigerate.

Next day, take the meat out of the sauce and set aside. Bring the sauce
to the boil and skim to remove any fat. Press the sauce though a fine
sieve, then whisk in the butter to shine and enrich it. Check the
seasoning. Add the beef to the sauce and simmer for 20 minutes to
reheat. Serve with fresh pasta or creamy mashed potato (see p. 159).

CHEESE AND HAM PIE

This is great as a main course or as a starter. It is best warm, but also very tasty served cold from the fridge. Good-quality bought puff pastry is fine if you don't want to make your own.

SERVES 6–8 AS A MAIN DISH
375g puff pastry
1 egg, beaten
50g mature Cheddar, grated
150g Gruyère or similar, grated
700g good-quality cooked ham, sliced thin
BÉCHAMEL SAUCE
25g butter
25g flour
150ml milk
50ml double cream
salt, pepper, nutmeg

First, make the béchamel by melting the butter in a saucepan until it foams. Mix in the flour and gently cook over a low heat for 4–5 minutes, not allowing it to colour. With the pan still on the heat, slowly whisk in the milk and cream, then increase the heat and bring to the boil. Keep mixing well to avoid lumps and burning – the sauce should be quite thick. Season lightly with salt but quite generously with pepper and nutmeg. Pour into a container and cover with a buttered paper to avoid a crust forming. Set the béchamel aside to cool down completely.

On a lightly floured surface, roll out half of the pastry to a rough circle, about 24cm wide. Roll out another circle about 26cm wide. Cover this one and keep it cold.

Preheat the oven to 200°C/Gas 6. Place the first pastry circle on a baking tray, brush the edges with beaten egg and put a spoonful of béchamel in the centre of the circle. Spread this over the pastry with a pallet knife or the back of the spoon to within 3-4cm of the edges. Sprinkle over a little cheese, followed by some ham. Repeat these layers until all the ham, cheese and béchamel have been used up.

Cover the filling with the other sheet of pastry and press down firmly around the edges to seal. Trim the edges neatly, brush with beaten egg and score the top with the point of a knife to decorate. Make a little hole in the centre of the top of the pie to let out the steam. Bake at 200°C/Gas 6 for 30 minutes, then turn the oven down to 180°C/Gas 4 and cook for another 15 minutes. Leave the pie to cool for at least 30 minutes before cutting into slices.

SLOW-ROAST LEG OF MUTTON WITH SUGAR AND SPICE

Mutton is such a lovely meat and this method of cooking it with the marinade ensures a moist, tender and hassle-free lunch. Mutton is much easier to find nowadays, but you could use mature, end-of-season lamb instead. Alternatively, buy your meat at a halal butcher. Halal meat is usually very good, with the strong flavour needed for this recipe.

SERVES 10–12

1 leg of mutton, about 3.2kg
2 cloves garlic
4 tablespoons olive oil
120g Greek yoghurt
2 tablespoons finely chopped fresh ginger
2 pinches saffron threads
1 teaspoon ground coriander seeds
1 teaspoon freshly milled black pepper
2 teaspoons salt
4 tablespoons light brown sugar
juice of 1 lemon
finely grated zest of ½ lemon,
1 teaspoon Madras curry powder
2 teaspoons dry chilli flakes
1 tablespoon tomato ketchup

Trim any excess fat off the leg of mutton, then using a darning needle or a long, thin-bladed knife, stab the leg about 12 times all over.

Peel and crush the garlic, then mix with all the other ingredients until smooth. Now take a little of the marinade and rub it over the meat. Place the mutton on an oiled roasting tray, rounded side up. Smear the rest of the marinade thickly on this side, lightly cover with clingfilm and refrigerate for at least 8 hours.

To cook, remove the clingfilm and place the mutton in the oven at 160°C/Gas 2–3 for 2 hours. Do not turn the leg over, but you may need to turn the roasting tray round if the meat is cooking more on one side than the other.

After the 2 hours have elapsed, turn the oven temperature up to 200°C/Gas 6 and cook for another 30 minutes. Keep an eye on the meat as some ovens go up in temperature quicker than others. The mutton should now be sizzling and have a lovely golden-brown crust. Switch the oven off and leave the meat as it is for another 30 minutes.

To serve, take the roast out and carve it straight from the oven. Collect the roasting pan juices to serve at the same time. Accompany with some light, fluffy basmati rice and a mixed salad.

GNOCCHI AND WILD MUSHROOM GRATIN

This particular type of gnocchi is made with choux pastry and is called 'à la Parisienne'. I used to make a dish similar to this when I worked as an apprentice in Paris. It is now a favourite in the Roux household as it's easy and fun to make.

SERVES 4–6

CHOUX PASTRY
250ml water
100g butter
1 pinch salt
1 pinch white pepper, ground
1 teaspoon dry cep powder
   (optional)
125g plain flour, sifted
3 free-range eggs

BÉCHAMEL SAUCE
30g butter
30g plain flour
350ml milk
salt, pepper, nutmeg
1 sprig thyme
1 bay leaf

FILLING AND TOPPING
360g mixed wild
   mushrooms
olive oil
2 cloves garlic, peeled
   and crushed
60g Cheddar, grated
40g Parmesan, grated

Start by making the choux pastry. Bring the water and butter to the boil with the seasoning. As soon as it boils, take the pan off the heat and stir in the sifted flour with a wooden spatula. When this is well mixed and smooth, return the pan to the heat. Cook the choux pastry over a medium flame, stirring vigorously all the time. Continue to cook for 2–3 minutes; the bottom should be starting to catch. Take the pan off the heat and beat in the eggs one at a time. This takes a long time and a lot of beating. *Continued overleaf*

Put the choux paste in a piping bag with an 8mm hole. Gently squeeze the bag over a pan of salted, boiling water, using a small, sharp knife to cut the paste into roughly 1cm lengths as it comes out. Simmer the gnocchi for about 5 minutes, then gently lift them out with a slotted spoon. Put them straight into iced water to halt the cooking, then drain in a colander.

Next make the béchamel. Melt the butter in a saucepan, add the flour and cook until foaming, but do not allow to colour. Slowly whisk in the milk over high heat and add the seasoning and herbs. Bring to the boil, then turn down the heat and simmer the sauce for 10 minutes. Take off the heat, pour through a fine sieve, cover and set aside.

Clean and trim the mushrooms. Pan fry in a little olive oil, allowing them to colour a little. Add the garlic at the end, season with salt and a little pepper.

Preheat the oven to 200°C/Gas 6. Take an ovenproof dish, measuring about 20 x 28cm and about 5cm deep, or some individual dishes. Scatter in the gnocchi and wild mushrooms, pour over the béchamel sauce and sprinkle with the cheese. Bake in the hot oven for 20 minutes until golden brown.

LEMON DELICE

caster sugar for sugar syrup
2 lemons, thinly sliced
sponge fingers (see p.309)
250ml lemon juice
250ml double cream
6 egg yolks
150g caster sugar
3 leaves of gelatine, soaked
250ml whipping cream, whipped
2 tablespoons vodka

Make a sugar syrup with equal quantities of sugar and water. Cook the lemon slices in the syrup for one hour at 105°C/Gas ¼ in the oven. Make some basic sponge fingers (see p. 309) and leave to cool.

Bring the lemon juice to the boil, add the cream and quickly bring back to the boil. Whisk the yolks and the 150g of caster sugar together until pale, then pour in the lemon and cream mixture. Mix well, then return to pan and cook until it thickens and coats the back of the spoon. Do not overcook or it will scramble.

Add the softened gelatine and pass the mixture through a fine sieve. When cold, but not set, fold in the whipped cream.

Line a charlotte mould with some of the lemon slices. Add a layer of sponge and soak it with some of the lemon sugar syrup and vodka. Pour in the lemon and cream mixture and then top with some more lemon slices.

SIX

Family and friends

My wife Gisele is as passionate about food and cooking as I am and she always has been. It's a very important part of our life together. When we first met, Gisele was working at Gavvers and Le Gamin as a manageress. She's from a very small village called Clairac, which is not far from Nîmes in southwest France. She'd come to London to learn English.

Our relationship was a bit difficult to begin with because Gisele was already married to a young chef. At the time he was working at Le Gamin and then he moved to Gavvers. And I was in a steady relationship, too. But their marriage was in the throes of breaking down and I guess a certain chemistry happens in love. We were lovers in this mad world of catering. We didn't keep it a secret for too long and quite soon it was open and above board.

At the time, however, it was quite difficult to explain the situation to our respective sets of parents, especially as we were all working together. But once we'd done that and they saw we were serious, my parents and Gisele's parents accepted it and we settled into our life together.

We didn't eat out that often. We went out to bars and the kinds of casual restaurants young people go to. We were interested in places that were hip, fun and young. Clubbing and pubbing about sums it up. But most of the time we were working through lunch and dinner, particularly when we were doing the catering part of the business. Because we worked such long hours, we often ate at home. Gisele makes a very good gratin dauphinois, which is a French staple. Very often we'd have this just with a salad, because it's almost a meal in itself.

I'm very fortunate to be married to Gisele, someone who knows the business and who's worked in it. Your partner has to understand the hours and the commitment. But we don't work together any more, which is another reason why we're still happily married.

The restaurant business has a high percentage of divorce and break-up and you can understand it. If you work together in the same premises, you often end up screaming and shouting at each other and you tend to take those arguments home.

There are also higher than average rates of alcoholism and drug abuse in the restaurant business. I've seen it all the way through my career. It's the extraordinary pressure and the fact that when you're working long hours you try to cram in more fun in a shorter time.

And we're in an environment of eating and drinking. Chefs work hard and they play hard. It's easy to see what happens. You work hard, you have a couple of drinks, and the couple of drinks leads to a couple more. You have very little sleep and then you need something to pep you up... and it snowballs. Before, it used to be just drink, but drugs are now readily available and it can be harder to tell what's going on with those than with alcohol. It's something I'm aware of as a boss these days.

Gratin dauphinois
SERVES 4

750g potatoes, such as Rooster or Maris Piper
1 clove garlic
350ml double cream
salt, pepper, nutmeg

Peel and thinly slice the potatoes, but do not wash them. Gently toss with the seasoning and cream. Rub the baking dish with the cut side of the garlic and then spread the potatoes and cream mix evenly in the dish, pressing down as you go. Cover with buttered foil and bake in the oven at 160°C/Gas 2–3 for 30 minutes. Remove the foil and turn up the heat to 200°C/Gas 6 for a further 15 minutes. Leave to cool for 10 minutes before serving.

If you haven't worked in the industry, you simply wouldn't understand. Gisele does know what it's like; she knows the industry and the pressures on everyone. One of the few times we did work together was when I was a young chef at La Tante Claire on Royal Hospital Road, where Gordon Ramsay is now. Gisele worked part-time there as a cashier in the evening.

My father had helped Pierre Koffmann find backers for La Tante Claire. He backed him as well and he thought it would be good for me to work there for a while. It would be a step up to work in a restaurant with two, soon to be three, Michelin-stars. Working with Pierre was an experience. He's an amazing character – a gentle giant, a gourmet and an extremely talented chef. But he can be a grumpy bear and he's not easy to work for. Although he's a massive, rugby-style man, he has a very delicate touch. He'd take massive turbots and instead of using a filleting knife, he'd use an enormous butcher's knife to cut them up. But he was so dexterous and skilled, he'd fillet the whole thing perfectly, with no waste at all. Likewise, he could bone a pig's trotter – no easy task – in less than a minute.

All his food was earthy and flavoursome. He's from the southwest of France so his dishes were robust and strong on flavour. In that way his food was different from Le Gavroche and he was a lot more straightforward in his style and approach. Talk about making money in a kitchen! He was, and still is, the most frugal man. Not a thing was wasted. It was either used in a stock or a sauce, or for the staff food. He'd go to the markets himself and buy seconds of fruit for making sorbets and ice creams. He ran a very tight ship. It was a small restaurant – 40 seats and a team of four in the kitchen – so it was all hands on deck. If the washing-up guy didn't show up, we just mucked in and did it ourselves.

At La Tante Claire, Pierre Koffmann once said to me that I didn't even peel an onion correctly. And he was right – I didn't. It always annoys me now when I see someone cut an onion in half and then peel it. Peel it first and then cut it. It's just basic efficiency. By all means question the rules when you're a young chef, but remember that most of the time, things are done a certain way for a reason.

I learned so much from Pierre, too – how to organise a kitchen and how to make money out of nothing. Pig's trotter stuffed with morels and sweetbreads was one of his signature dishes and he made his own filo pastry for his version of apple strudel. We used to make that in the afternoon on a big table and pull it out until it was transparent. Once the pastry was stretched out you had to cut it into sheets immediately before it dried out.

It was a very good time in my life. I loved my work, and Gisele and I were happy and very much in love. We rented a flat in Clapham from my uncle and that summer we went to Ireland for a fishing holiday with my parents, back to Cahersiveen. It was a kind of pilgrimage, and we went back to the same place. It was just the same, great fishing, great fun and that amazing Irish hospitality.

Grilled saffron milk-caps

Depending on the weather, saffron milk-caps make their appearance from July to August, normally just before the first boletes or ceps. My brother-in-law Gérard and his son Julien always find them in the pine forests of the Cévennes. They always thought of milk-caps as rather tasteless, worthless mushrooms until I showed them how to cook them.

Take your mushrooms and brush away any dirt and pine needles. Trim if necessary. Grill over hot coals on the barbecue. Tie a bundle of thyme together to make a brush, then use this to baste the mushrooms with a little olive oil. Cook for a few minutes, then sprinkle with sea salt and coarsely ground pepper.

HAUNCH OF VENISON
WITH LEMON AND HONEY

SERVES 8

leg of venison, about 3kg
olive oil
juice of 1 lemon
4 tablespoons clear honey
4 onions
1 large or 2 small lemons
sprig of thyme
white wine
salt, pepper

Rub the venison leg with a little olive oil, salt, pepper, lemon juice and 1 tablespoon of honey. Cover with clingfilm and leave to marinate overnight.

Preheat the oven to 220°C/Gas 7. Heat up a roasting tray on top of the stove and sear the venison with a good bit of olive oil. Once the meat is coloured on all sides, put it in the hot oven for 10 minutes.

Then add the coarsely sliced onions, the lemons cut into wedges, 3 tablespoons of honey, thyme and a good glass of white wine. Put the meat back in the oven at 180°C/Gas 4 for 30 minutes. Then turn the heat off and leave the venison in the oven for a further 30 minutes. Remove and take to the table to carve.

DUCK CONFIT

SERVES 8
8 duck legs
500g good-quality coarse sea salt
1.5kg duck fat
1 sprig thyme
6 sage leaves

Liberally sprinkle the salt over the duck legs and refrigerate for 90 minutes. Then brush off the salt with a cloth and discard.

Warm the duck fat in a pan over low heat. Add the duck legs and the thyme and sage. Bring to a very gentle simmer, cover with greaseproof paper and cook for 2 hours or until tender. The slower and longer the cooking time, the better the duck will be. Leave to cool in the fat and then refrigerate. The confit will keep for several weeks.

When you want to eat the confit, gently lift the legs out of the fat and place skin-side down in a non-stick pan. Cook over medium heat until crispy and golden. Turn the legs over and put in preheated oven at 180°C/Gas 4 to finish warming through for 10–15 minutes. Serve with sauté potatoes (see p. 159).

WILD BOAR WITH CHESTNUTS AND QUINCE

My brother-in-law Gérard and his son Julien are both very keen hunters and during the game season they regularly shoot wild boar and deer in the mountains of the Cévennes and Ardèche. They make pâtés and terrines with the heads, then use the shoulders for stews and the chops for the barbecue. Ribs and belly are salted and air-dried, and sausages are made with special spices. The liver, heart and kidneys are also given special treatment.

SERVES 10–12

shoulder of boar, about 4kg
olive oil
salt, pepper
onions
garlic
bay leaf

quince, peeled and chopped
wine
1 tablespoon quince paste
about 20 chestnuts, cooked
  and peeled

Using a boning knife, cut into the two joints of the shoulder. Go in far enough to loosen but not separate them. Place the meat in a large cast-iron dish with a splash of olive oil. Season well with salt and pepper and cook in a hot oven at 200°C/Gas 6 for 20 minutes.

Add the sliced onions, garlic, bay leaf and quince, and enough wine (rosé is good) to wet the base of the dish. Add the same amount of water, cover with foil and turn the oven down to 150°C/Gas 2 for 1 hour. The meat should be soft and coming off the bone.

Using a slotted spoon, gently take out the meat and place it in a deep serving dish. Cover and keep warm. Put the cooking dish over a high heat and add a glass of water (or vegetable stock), quince paste and the chestnuts. Simmer for 5 minutes to melt the quince paste, pour over the meat and serve.

LAMB PIES

SERVES 12
500g plain flour
500ml water
5g yeast
170g butter, melted
3 egg yolks
1 teaspoon salt
1 tablespoon sugar
350g plain flour
FILLING
600g leftover braised lamb shoulder
  or boiled mutton
4 hard-boiled eggs, chopped
1 egg, beaten

Mix together the 500g of flour with the water and yeast. Cover and leave to rise and double in volume.

Then mix in the melted butter, egg yolks, salt, sugar and the 350g of flour. Mix until smooth, then cover and refrigerate for 6 hours.

Roll the dough out to a thickness of about 1cm, then cut out discs measuring 8cm across. Shred the lamb and fold in the chopped egg. Divide the filling into 8 and place some in the centre of each pastry disc. Moisten the edges of the pastry with a little beaten egg and then fold over, pressing down the edges to seal. Place the pies on a baking sheet and leave to rise for 20 minutes. Brush with beaten egg and cook at 200°C/Gas 6 for 15 minutes.

ALAIN CHAPEL'S TOURTE DE CHEVREUIL
HOT VENISON PIES

SERVES 20

1kg venison meat, trimmed

300g fatty pork meat

300g veal

800g pork fat

2 tablespoons brandy

salt, pepper,

2kg puff pastry

beaten egg

FARCE À GRATIN

150g venison liver

100g raw foie gras

1 tablespoon duck fat

2 shallots, chopped

1 sprig thyme

1 bay leaf

2 tablespoons brandy

First make the 'farce à gratin' – if you can't get venison liver you can use chicken livers. Sear the liver and raw foie gras in a very hot frying pan with the duck fat. After a few seconds, add the chopped shallots, thyme and bay leaf, then season well. When the livers are still very pink, add the brandy and take off the heat. Press all this, including the liquid, though a coarse drum sieve, and set aside.

Cut all the other meats and fat into small chunks, season with salt, pepper, cover and refrigerate overnight. Next day, mince using a hand mincer with a 5mm size disc. It is best to refrigerate the mincer before using to keep everything as cold as possible. Once this is done, add the farce à gratin, seasoning and brandy. Shape the mixture into small balls weighing about 120g.

Line buttered rings, about 8cm across, with pastry and put a ball of meat mixture in each one. Top with discs of pastry. Make a hole in the top of each pie and insert a roll of greaseproof as a chimney to let the steam out during cooking. Brush with beaten egg and bake at 180°C/Gas 4 for 20 minutes.

A great moment
on a fishing holiday
in Australia.

By this time, Gisele and my parents got on well, but I'd never met
Gisele's family, so later that year we went to see them in France.
It was pretty nerve-wracking for me and I was very apprehensive.
But we got over any initial difficulties, perhaps because we all
loved food so much. Gisele's family really enjoy their food. They
used to rear rabbits for the table, chickens for eating and for eggs,
and they had a huge vegetable garden. Sadly, Marcel, Gisele's father,
has died, but her mother, Raymonde, still grows her own fruit and
vegetables, even though she's now in her eighties. She still has an
unbelievable appetite, too.

Gisele grew up in the Cévennes region, which is very hilly and
known for its wild mushrooms and chestnuts. It's an old coal-
mining area, with lots of rivers running through it. It's a rugged
landscape – dry and arid in summer and lots of rain in winter.

Her family ate very much in the traditional way. When everyone
was together, there would always be a feast – three or four starters,
such as some sort of fish, pâté and charcuterie, followed by a hot

dish. The meals were epic. They went on forever. While we were there, Gisele and I used to fish for crayfish in the Gardon. We'd go out at 1 or 2 in the morning and walk barefoot upstream. We'd shine our torch down into the water and pick up the crayfish with our hands. The rivers were clear and shallow and you could see the crayfish very clearly. We used to get frogs as well and we'd go back to the house with a big haul of food.

Raymonde would cook the crayfish in a tomato sauce, the traditional way in that region, with a bit of chilli, loads of garlic, olive oil and a bit of dried sausage. And we'd dive in, and eat the crayfish with our hands. They were fantastic.

When Marcel was alive, he'd kill a chicken or a cockerel each week for the table. He'd bleed it of course and pour the blood into

---

Ecrevisse à la tomate
Crayfish in tomato sauce
SERVES 4

24 small live crayfish
4 shallots, peeled and sliced
4 cloves garlic, peeled and chopped
4 tablespoons olive oil
120g saucisson sec (salami)
600g fresh tomatoes, skinned, seeded and chopped
2 bay leaves
2 sprigs thyme
2 small dry chillies
1 glass dry white wine
salt

Remove the digestive tracts from the crayfish by pulling out the middle tail fin. Cook the shallots and garlic in a little olive oil over a high heat until starting to colour. Add the crayfish, stir, then cover with a lid and continue to cook. After 2–3 minutes, add the diced salami and all the remaining ingredients. Stir well, season and simmer for 15 minutes. Allow to cool a little before devouring with your fingers.

a dish to which was added big crumbs of stale bread, chopped parsley, chopped garlic and olive oil. It was then cooked like a pancake. It sounds revolting, but it was absolutely delicious. It's called sanguette, or blood pancake.

Then we'd have roast chicken, always roasted with the head and comb still on. Raymonde still loves to crack the chicken head open, tease out the brains and eat them – chicken brains are a great delicacy. The skin gets very crackly on the head and the neck, and it tastes so good – fiddly to eat but delicious. When I was at La Tante Claire, we often used to serve chicken or duck necks for the staff lunch. They're a bit like spare ribs.

I loved working at La Tante Claire and I had enormous respect and affection for Pierre. But then an opportunity arose for me to do work experience at The Mandarin Hotel in Hong Kong and I jumped at it. To work in a great hotel and see how it functioned was a fantastic opportunity, but of course I wanted Gisele to come too. There was no way I was going to spend three months without her.

Sanguette
Blood pancake

Collect the blood from a freshly killed rooster or chicken. You can also use 125ml of pigs' blood if available. To this add a handful of dry baguette crumbs. They must be big and coarse, not fine. Add a tablespoon of roughly chopped flat-leaf parsley, a clove of chopped garlic, salt and pepper.

Heat up a cast-iron pan with a tablespoon of olive oil. When smoking hot, pour the mixture into the pan and cook like an omelette. Flip over and cook the other side. Delicious served hot or cold, for breakfast or for a snack.

Gisele and I at a cocktail reception just before leaving for Hong Kong.

So we sorted out the paperwork and figured that, although I was on work experience and therefore not earning very much, we'd still have enough to live on in a modest way. For some reason, we travelled there on two different planes. I arrived about an hour earlier and waited and waited, not knowing that she'd been stopped at immigration and was being questioned about where she was staying and how she was going to support herself. And although everything Gisele said was true, they interrogated her for hours before they finally let her out. It wasn't the best start to our time there, but the Mandarin put us up for two weeks free of charge and then we had to find somewhere to live.

It was practically impossible to find somewhere affordable and in the end we found a single room in an apartment in the Aberdeen area of Hong Kong, which was rented by another cook at the hotel. It was a box room with no window, no air conditioning and a single bed. We lived there for a month, before we were able to move into a larger room in the same apartment. Fortunately, I love the heat. We both do. I'd far rather be in 40-plus degrees than zero degrees. I feel far more at ease in hot weather than in cold.

Gisele couldn't work there, although she did some babysitting and she taught French. She would go to the local markets every day and get fresh tofu and vegetables. Gisele is a great one for a bargain. Unbelievably she'd haggle like hell over the price of tofu, and get it for about five pence instead of ten. We had no money, but it was great fun. And there was no way I would ask my parents for help, no way at all. We ate in the noodle bar at the bottom of the apartment block, or at the street stalls. We went native, totally native. Sometimes we'd take the ferry over to one of the islands and eat great dishes of clams with black bean sauce and plain steamed rice.

The experience of cooking in the kitchens there was pretty amazing. At that time the Mandarin was regarded as one the best hotels in the world and it had a world-class gastronomic restaurant – The Pierrot. If that restaurant had been in France or London, it definitely would have had three Michelin stars. The food there was wonderful and I knew the maître d', Philippe Requin, from Le Poulbot in London. He was a very impressive worker. In just 18 months, he'd risen from basic waiter to assistant manager.

Like all hotels of that type, the Mandarin had seasons with guest chefs. Roger Vergé came and I worked with his team for ten days, and my uncle came over for ten days to do a Waterside Inn promotion. Then I finally worked with my old boss Marcel Le Serveau from the Elysée Palace when he did a gastronomic week at the Mandarin. It was wonderful to see him again.

There was also a fantastic Grill Room, a coffee shop and a highly regarded Chinese restaurant called the Man Wah. I spent time in the Chinese restaurant, although the Chinese chefs were quite suspicious of me. I tried to break the ice by bringing in beer and inviting them out for a drink. It helped a little, but there were still language difficulties.

Like many Chinese, the chef at the Man Wah was a very keen gambler. I remember him shouting and bobbing his head up and down as he cooked. I thought this was bizarre until I realised he had a little aerial sticking out of his hat and an earpiece in his ear. He was listening to the races!

OPPOSITE: In the kitchens at the Mandarin, Hong Kong. Shopping at the local street markets.

I saw some fantastic food there – they'd build barbecues right on the kitchen floor for suckling pig. I saw whole heron being cooked. They never actually ate the heron, but made a broth out of it. It was cooked twice in its own stock with various herbs and

then a beautifully clear soup was decanted. The only parts of the bird that were kept were its feet. Everything else was thrown away. The soup tasted amazing – very intense.

They also baked chicken in clay – they shaped the clay round the chicken, roasted it and then cracked it open at the table. And they made the most wonderful platters of cold meats and vegetables. They'd spend hours arranging all these bits and pieces on the plate and it ended up looking like the most beautiful tapestry. As for the Grill Room – I've never seen anything like it. You'd walk in and see the most enormous display of fish and meat from all over the world. On Sundays they'd serve fantastic roasts.

On my days off, I'd quite often knock on the doors of restaurants where we'd eaten and ask if I could see how they cooked. There was one restaurant called Pep'N Chilli, which served the most wonderful lobster with chilli, and I finally talked my way into the kitchen. They wouldn't let me touch anything, but I was able to see a little of how they worked. Of course, they were quite secretive and suspicious, even though I brought in the beers! I was intrigued by their knowledge of spices and the way they combined sugar and salt. They've always done that, but it's now very fashionable in the West – salted caramel, salt in the chocolate. It's not new, but it's new to our taste buds. Sugar and chilli also work well together.

We came back from Hong Kong in 1984, and I went to work in the outside catering business again. I loved my time in Hong Kong, but realistically I knew there was no way I could turn it into a permanent job because it was only work experience. In many ways it was unfinished business, because I could have learned so much more. And I love good hotels.

Gisele and I were together for six or seven years before we married. We got married in 1990 and Emily was born in 1991. We'd been trying for a child for many years before that, and for a long time Gisele didn't want to be married because we didn't have a child. But we got married and had IVF treatment– Emily is among the first test-tube babies. Gisele became pregnant on the fourth attempt, and we got our lovely baby girl.

Our wedding day in the Seychelles. Emily with her first birthday cake.

We eloped. We flew off to the Seychelles, to the Plantation Club on Mahé Island. We arranged to fly on April 1, April Fool's Day, to be married on the beach. Gisele was working at our head office on Wandsworth Road then, and the travel company making the arrangements rang and asked to speak to Mr Roux. My father took the call and he was asked all these questions about a forthcoming wedding! So my parents knew the day before, but really we wanted it to be a secret. We wanted to fly off and get married, and then tell everyone after the event.

We were totally on our own. Gisele had the travel company rep as her witness and I chose the barman, who is now the head of the Seychelles cooking and service industries school. We're still frequent visitors to the Seychelles, particularly to Bird Island. That to me is paradise. There are no phones, no computers, no television, except in the office. You get off a little plane and you switch off completely. There are just 24 bungalows and the food is fantastic. Everyone eats from a buffet at the same time.

Emily goes with us as well and we go fishing from a boat or on the beach. Emily never lets me forget the time we were fishing on the beach and I caught a big one, but got it snagged on a rock. So I asked her to swim out, follow the line and unsnag the fish.

She didn't want to because it was getting dark. Then the fish somehow freed itself and I landed it. It was a huge ray, with big stingers and Emily always teases me about the time I wanted to make her swim into danger. The hotel manager came down to the beach to see if we wanted the kitchen to cook the ray. But I let it back into the sea to fight another day.

Other holidays are spent at our house in France. My home in France is my bolt hole. I go there to relax, chill out and cook for my friends and family. I have a cellar that is stocked with wines from all over the world – the locals are always curious about these, but they enjoy the choice I offer. I do, of course, drink the local wines too, and there are many very good ones.

Our village is typical of *La France profonde* – 'Deep France'. There's a church, two bakers, a butcher, a tabac and three bars. The old boys drink pastis and play pétanque, while the ladies sit on the bench chatting away about whatever old ladies chat about. I love the leisurely pace, the fact that everyone says bonjour when we cross the street or enter a shop, and that people are just so genuine. The local produce is an inspiration. The market stalls are always brimming with fresh seasonal food, everything from goat's cheese to just-picked ripe peaches. And then there is the local truffle gatherer who knocks at my door – always at aperitif time, of course – offering some gnarly black diamonds ready to be grated on some scrambled eggs.

In the summer months, a walk through the vineyards or orchards followed by a swim in the river, is a perfect way to work up an appetite. In the winter, when the cold mistral blows, the roaring fire beckons and a few roasted chestnuts with a glass or two of wine is really all that's needed.

Those times on holiday are particularly important to me because I work so hard. We all do, so holidays and home are extra special. We always eat simply at home, but we take our time and enjoy our meals for what they are. It's one of the reasons my wife and I get on so well because we both recognise that a simple meal made with good basic ingredients can be just as rewarding as dinner in a three-star restaurant.

CLOCKWISE FROM TOP LEFT: Looking out over the River Ardèche. Sampling the local wine, Domaine Galety. Shopping for goat cheese in the market with Gisele. Mathieu, the truffle hunter, with his dog Nora. The ladies of the village.

WARM ROASTED VEGETABLE SALAD, WITH RASPBERRY VINEGAR AND ALMOND OIL

Make sure to find a good-quality raspberry vinegar and toasted almond oil for this salad. You can also use argan or hazelnut oil instead of almond – the choice is yours.

SERVES 6

2 thick slices white bread
olive oil for frying
1 medium carrot
1 medium parsnip
½ celeriac
1 beetroot, cooked
8 shiitake mushrooms
8 chestnuts, cooked
2 spring onions
½ bunch flat-leaf parsley, picked and washed
250g lollo rosso and frisée salad leaves, picked and washed
1 Granny Smith apple
4 tablespoons raspberry vinegar
8 tablespoons almond oil
salt, pepper

Remove the crusts from the bread and discard. Cut the bread into 1cm squares and gently fry them in a non-stick pan with a little olive oil until crisp and golden. Drain and season with a little salt.

Peel the carrot, parsnip and celeriac and cut into small batons about 3cm long x ½cm thick. Blanch in salted, boiling water for 1 minute, and then lift out with a slotted spoon and put in iced water to halt the cooking. Drain well when cool. Cut the beetroot into similar-sized batons and slice the mushrooms. Peel the chestnuts and break into large crumbs. Thinly slice the spring onions, using the white and green, and put with the salad leaves and parsley.

In a large non-stick pan, start to pan fry the carrots, celeriac, mushrooms and parsnips with a drizzle of olive oil. Keep tossing them around to get an even colour – this should take about 5 minutes. Now add the beetroot and chestnuts and continue to cook for another 2–3 minutes. Peel and cut the apple into batons the same size as the vegetables. (This can be done in advance and the batons placed in a little cold water with lemon juice so they don't go brown.)

Mix the almond oil and raspberry vinegar. Season the salad with a little salt and pepper and add the apple batons and toasted bread. Toss well, using about one-third of the dressing. Put the remaining vinaigrette into the pan with the vegetables and season. Serve the vegetables on individual warmed plates, with the salad on top, and drizzle any vinaigrette left in the pan around the salad.

BAKED EGGS WITH HAM AND TRUFFLE

Truffles are an extravagant luxury but well worth saving-up for. Make sure you buy the most fragrant, ripe, winter truffles. The black Périgord truffle (*Tuber melanosporum*) is usually at its best from January to March. The truffle should be tender to touch and jet black. Place it in an airtight container with the eggs and keep refrigerated for at least 3 days before using. As the shells of the eggs are porous, they take on the scent of the truffle.

SERVES 4

butter
1 truffle, about 40g
4 thin slices of good-quality air-dried ham, such as Parma
200ml crème fraîche
salt, pepper
4 free-range eggs
brioche

Take 4 ovenproof glass or porcelain ramekin dishes, big and deep enough to take an egg and 2 tablespoons of cream. Butter the dishes with a pastry brush.

Preheat the oven to 150°C/Gas 2. Slice the truffle thinly, using a small, sharp knife or a truffle slicer. Carefully place truffle slices around the inside of each dish. Cut the ham slices into strips and put a little in each dish. Add a spoonful of cream, more ham, any truffle that's left over, and then the remaining cream. Season lightly, then carefully break an egg on top of the cream in each ramekin.

Bake in a water bath in the preheated oven for about 10 minutes. The whites of the eggs should be set and the yolks still a little runny. Finish with a sprinkle of salt and pepper and serve with some toasted brioche.

PUMPKIN AND SWEDE CRUMBLE

This is a delicious winter dish which needs no accompaniment – it is a meal itself. The crumble can be made in advance and stored in an airtight container in the fridge. The pumpkin mix can also be made beforehand and simply sprinkled with the crumble before baking.

SERVES 6–8

100g butter, cold
150g plain flour, sifted
1 heaped teaspoon Maldon sea salt
100g Cheddar cheese, grated
75g almonds, hazelnuts or walnuts, chopped
300g pumpkin
300g swede
300g butternut squash (peeled weight)
2 tablespoons olive oil
1 medium onion, chopped
salt, pepper, nutmeg
2 sprigs rosemary
2 cloves garlic, finely chopped
BALSAMIC DRESSING
30ml balsamic vinegar
1 teaspoon demerara sugar
2 tablespoons olive oil
salt, pepper
1 tablespoon Dijon wholegrain mustard

To make the crumble topping, work the cold butter into the sifted flour using your fingertips. Then gently rub between your hands to obtain a sandy, coarse crumb. Add the salt, cheese and nuts, but do not over mix. The texture should stay very loose and sandy. Set aside until needed.

Cut the pumpkin, swede and squash into bite-sized chunks and place them in a heavy-based saucepan with the olive oil. Cook over a high heat, stirring occasionally until the vegetables start to take on a little colour. Turn the heat down to moderate, add the chopped onion, seasoning and rosemary. Cover with a piece of foil and continue to cook for 20 minutes, or until tender. Now stir in the finely chopped garlic and continue to cook for another 10 minutes.

Remove the rosemary and pour the vegetables into an earthenware or ovenproof dish – this should have a depth of 4cm and be big enough to take all the mixture. Sprinkle the crumble mix evenly over the vegetables and bake in a preheated oven at 180°C/Gas 4 for 20 minutes until crisp and golden.

To make the dressing, simply mix all the ingredients together. Serve the dressing with the crumble.

CHERRY SOUP

Served hot or cold, this is a tangy refreshing classic.
Great served with smoked meats or foie gras.

SERVES 4

450g cherries
350ml water
200ml red wine
50ml port
1 stick cinnamon
peel of 1 lemon, cut into thin strips
½ tablespoon caster sugar
salt and pepper
½ the cherry stones crushed
1 tablespoon Kirsch

Stone the cherries. Keep a few back for the garnish and boil the rest in the water for 5–6 minutes. Set aside. Crush the stones of half the cherries and set aside.

Bring the wine and port to a boil and add the remaining ingredients including the crushed cherry stones. Cover and leave to steep until cool. Strain the liquid, add to the boiled cherries and blend until smooth. Season to taste.

The consistency may vary according to how much moisture there is in the cherries. If the soup is too thick, add a little water. It may also need a drop of lemon juice to balance the sweetness.

BROAD BEAN AND CHICKPEA SALAD

SERVES 4
1kg broad beans
180g cooked chickpeas (canned)
1 medium red onion
1 sprig of mint
2 tablespoons olive oil
1 tablespoon sesame oil
2 tablespoons sherry vinegar
green Tabasco
salt, pepper

Shell the broad beans and cook them in salted, boiling water for 3–4 minutes or until tender. Drain and place in iced water to halt the cooking and fix the colour. When the beans are cold, drain and remove the outer skins by gently pressing to coax out the tender vibrant green bean inside.

Drain and rinse the chickpeas. Peel the onion, cut it in half and slice thinly. Coarsely chop the mint. Toss all the ingredients together with the oils and vinegar, then season with the salt, pepper and Tabasco.

SALTED ALMOND CHOCOLATE TERRINE

This is rich, dark and delicious. And it is easy to make as there is no baking involved.

SERVES 8

200g sultanas
2 tablespoons dark rum
400g extra bitter chocolate (Valrhona or Amadei)
250g butter
150g golden syrup
2 eggs
100g good-quality salted almonds, left whole
100g digestive biscuits

Put the sultanas in a saucepan, cover with cold water and quickly bring to the boil. Drain and put the sultanas back in the pan. Add the rum, cover and leave to cool.

Melt the chocolate gently in the microwave or in a bowl over simmering water. Melt the butter and golden syrup together. Once everything is melted, slowly mix them together and add the eggs. Fold in the sultanas, with any rum remaining, the almonds and broken-up biscuits.

Pour the mixture into a terrine lined with clingfilm. Refrigerate for at least 6 hours or overnight, before slicing with a hot knife.

CHERRY CAKE

This cake can be made with any kind of berries, or even slices of pre-cooked apple, but cherry is my favourite. It's always worthwhile taking the time to stone the cherries first.

SERVES 8

120g unsalted butter, room temperature
120g caster sugar
2 large eggs
160g self-raising flour, sifted
1 tablespoon Kirsch
1 teaspoon vanilla extract
3 tablespoons milk
220g cherries

Butter a round cake tin with a diameter of 22cm. Preheat the oven to 180°C/Gas 4. Cream the butter and sugar in a mixing bowl until pale. Gradually mix in the eggs, followed by the flour, Kirsch, vanilla and milk. Gently fold in the fruit.

Pour the mixture into the cake tin and bake for 30-40 minutes. Check if the cake is done by inserting a needle or small knife into the centre – it should come out clean. Leave the cake to cool a little before removing it from the tin.

What I eat at home

Last Sunday night at home, Emily cooked. We had little crottin goat cheeses, with streaky bacon wrapped around each one. They were just put under the grill and we had two each. Then she made Thai spring rolls, using that rice paper you just dip in water. She rolled them up with batons of raw carrot, cucumber, cooked prawns, mint leaves and a bit of plum sauce. We had a mixed salad, some bread and a glass of rosé. It was delicious.

All our family meals are simple and very often we'll all muck in. We never sit down to a three- or four-course meal. But there's always fresh vegetables, fresh fruit, a salad and some meat, fish or cheese, and a glass of wine. Often we'll have pasta – packet pasta. The vast majority of pasta consumed in Italy is dried and there is absolutely nothing wrong with a good-quality dried pasta.

If we have steak, it will be grilled simply. Everything is simple and we sit together to eat. A good meal doesn't need lots of embellishments and it doesn't need to take huge amounts of time. And you don't need fancy expensive stoves. We've just had an induction hob put in, which is very good once you get used to it, and in France we have an Aga. Often people who spend huge amounts of money on stoves and other kitchen equipment are completely missing the point that eating at home should be simple and enjoyable.

OPPOSITE: At home with my wife and daughter – my favourite cooking companions.

FRIED BANANAS AND RUM

A fast and delicious dessert that everyone likes. We often make these on the spur of the moment to satisfy the craving for a sweet end to an informal family meal. Emily uses less butter and rum than I do, but the important thing is not to burn the caramel.

SERVES 3

1 tablespoon butter
3 bananas, skinned
2 tablespoons caster sugar
lemon
dark rum

Melt the butter in a large, non-stick pan. When it's frothy, add the skinned bananas. Turn them when they have started to take on a brown colour.

Now sprinkle on the caster sugar and gently swirl the pan to help the sugar mix and melt. Turn the bananas once more and lower the heat. The caramel and bananas should now be golden brown. Add a squeeze of lemon and a very generous splash of good dark rum. Flambé and bring to the table immediately. These are best served with some good-quality ice cream – from a tub, of course!

FRESH CHERRY CLAFOUTIS

SERVES 8

220g unsalted butter
200g sugar
pinch of vanilla sugar
4 eggs
grated zest of ½ lemon
100g flour
1 teaspoon baking powder
pinch of salt
120g ground almonds
2 tablespoons Kirsch
3 drops almond essence
500g cherries, stoned

Grease and flour a 22cm cake tin. Preheat the oven to 180°C/Gas 4.

Cream the butter and sugars in a mixing bowl until pale. Add the eggs one by one, followed by the lemon zest. Sift the flour with the baking powder and salt and fold into the mixture. Then gently fold in the ground almonds, Kirsch and almond essence. Finally, add half the cherries and pour the mixture into the tin. Poke the rest of the cherries into the top of the mixture.

Bake for 50 minutes in the preheated oven. Leave to cool in the tin for a short while before serving.

VANILLA DOUGHNUTS

These doughnuts will keep for a few days, but in my experience, they are usually gone within minutes. You can pipe a little blob of jam inside, using a piping bag and nozzle, or even dip them in chocolate. However, in my view, a dusting of vanilla-scented sugar is the best.

MAKES 36 SMALL DOUGHNUTS
225g strong white flour
1 teaspoon salt
15g yeast
25g caster sugar
25g butter
1 whole egg
80ml water
vegetable oil
vanilla sugar for dusting (see p. 307)

Put all the ingredients, except the oil and vanilla sugar, in the bowl of a food mixer with the dough hook attachment. Knead at low speed for 5 minutes, scraping down the edges when necessary to ensure a smooth and homogeneous dough. Then increase the speed to medium for 1 more minute. Cover and leave to rise for 20 minutes.

Knock the dough back and shape into little balls, approximately 10g each. Place these on a lightly oiled tray and cover with a cloth to keep them from drying out and getting a skin. Leave for 5–10 minutes to rise again. Heat the vegetable oil to 180°C and gently drop in the doughnuts, turning them when necessary. Once golden and puffed up, drain and roll in the vanilla sugar.

CHELSEA BUNS

We all love baking in our family. These little buns are gloriously delicious and can be eaten straight from the oven or lightly toasted with a slab of Brittany salted butter.

MAKES 15 BUNS

500g strong bread flour
75g caster sugar
1 teaspoon salt
75g butter
35g yeast
250ml milk, tepid

1 egg
grated zest of ½ lemon
50g sultanas
50g butter melted
½ tablespoon cinnamon
½ tablespoon icing sugar

Sift the flour, sugar and salt together, then gently rub in the butter. Dissolve the yeast in the tepid milk and add the egg. Gradually mix this with the flour until you have a dough texture – dust the work surface with extra flour to avoid it sticking. Place the dough in a bowl, cover and leave to prove until it has doubled in size.

Knock the dough back and roll out into a rectangle measuring about 20 x 40 cm. Brush with the melted butter and sprinkle with the sultanas and lemon zest. Mix together the cinnamon and icing sugar and sprinkle over the dough. Roll up the dough, starting from the longest edge, and cut the roll into about 15 pieces. Place the buns on a non-stick baking tray, making sure they are not too close together. Leave to rise for 15–20 minutes.

Cook in a hot oven, 220°C/Gas 7 for 15 minutes. The buns should be golden brown, yet moist, and all stuck together. Leave to cool a little on a wire rack before separating.

CHOCOLATE COOKIES

I love these cookies. They are not too sweet, and once cooked
they look like slices of black pudding! A great tasty joke.

MAKES ABOUT 30

125g butter, room temperature
1 egg yolk
60g soft brown sugar
1 tablespoon honey
1 pinch salt
130g flour, sifted
3 tablespoons pure cacao powder
1 pinch baking powder
100g white chocolate, cut into chips or nibs

Using your fingertips, mix the butter, egg yolk,
sugar, honey and salt together until smooth.
Then gradually add the sifted flour, cacao powder
and baking powder. Do not overwork. Quickly add
the white chocolate nibs. Roll the mixture into
cylinders about 3cm in diameter, then refrigerate.

When the cylinders are set, cut into 5mm slices
and place on a non-stick baking sheet. Cook in
a preheated oven at 180°C/Gas 4 for 15 minutes.
Leave to cool before eating.

EMILY'S WARM RUNNY CHOCOLATE PUDS

Emily my daughter often makes this dessert at home for us and it never fails to impress. The puddings can be made in advance, kept in the fridge for up to 6 hours, then cooked when you want them. We normally eat these with a good spoonful of crème fraîche, but during the summer season, fresh raspberries go beautifully.

SERVES 4

125g butter
125g best-quality, extra-bitter chocolate
3 eggs
2 tablespoons plain flour, sifted
125g caster sugar

Lightly butter 4 deep ramekins or ovenproof dishes, about 8 x 6cm. Melt the butter and chocolate in the microwave or in a bowl over a pan of simmering water.

Whisk the eggs, sugar and flour together until just mixed – don't worry about the odd lump or two! Pour the chocolate and butter into the egg mixture and fold together. Pour this into the moulds and then cook or refrigerate until needed.

If cooking immediately, place in a preheated oven at 180°C/Gas 4 for 10 minutes. (If cooking from the fridge, add 2 minutes to the cooking time.) Leave to rest for 1 minute, then serve. You can eat them straight from the dish or gently turn them out. Either way the centres should be hot and very runny.

SEVEN

Chef!

It was quite something to take over Le Gavroche. It's not just any restaurant and it wasn't just any chef's job. It still amazes me, even now, that so many people think of the Roux name as being synonymous with cooking greatness and a certain standard; how so many people are in awe of my father, my uncle and the Roux name. It's hard for me because Albert is, after all, my father and Michel is my uncle. And sometimes people even recognise me in the street. It's a bit embarrassing really because in many ways I'm not a famous person, and although my father enjoys being famous, being in the limelight and all the associated trappings, he never set out in life thinking he would achieve that much.

It's difficult to pinpoint a time when I realised how others regarded him. I suppose it would have coincided with the three Michelin stars. Moving to Mayfair brought a certain kudos and recognition that the Roux brothers were now in the West End. And when I was working in France, fellow chefs would say, 'He's the son of the famous Roux brothers.' That meant more to me, because it was recognition from peers abroad.

There was a huge amount of respect for the Roux name all over France. It's seen as a gold standard in the industry and my father and uncle are seen as pioneers of truly great French food. They're father and uncle to me, and their styles are quite different. If you were to compare them, my father is more of a baker and my uncle is more of an artist. My father is more into the heavy work – baking, kneading and making rich stews. My uncle is an extremely gifted artist with a very delicate touch. It shows in his work. A lot of his food is very refined, infinitely detailed and very precise. I enjoy his food and the way he cooks, but my father has a heartier approach. He's the sort of person who would be braising the whole joint of meat. Michel would be doing something with portions of it. So the two together were a natural recipe for success. I'd like to think I'm a fusion of them both, because I do like precision. But perhaps I lean a bit towards my father's homely, flavoursome, straightforward approach to food.

Certainly it was a help in the beginning for my father to make those phone calls and pull a few strings. I wouldn't have got into the Elysée Palace without him. But when I was an apprentice and just starting out, even when I was at La Tante Claire, people would point out that I'd had it so easy and they'd almost wait for me to fail. It wasn't bullying as such, but it came quite close to it. If they could stab me in the back they would.

Taking over Le Gavroche in the early 1990s was hard – probably the toughest time in my life. As well as finding my feet and getting everything going, we almost immediately ran into a recession. Many people think restaurants like Le Gavroche are immune, but this is just not true, especially in a recession like the one in the late '80s and early '90s, which lasted for a long time. We had to lay off staff and the rest of us had to work twice as hard. And mentally, it was tough. But when I look back, I would have done all the same things.

Sometimes I've thought that I should have changed everything when I took over, completely changed it. But finally I had too much respect for Le Gavroche. It had such a name and such a following. It was a massive weight on my shoulders to keep it going. And if I'd changed it completely, I would have been vilified. But I still got it in the neck for keeping it going.

I feel very strongly about Le Gavroche and what it has been and what it must continue to be – very individual, different to any other restaurant in town, and offering the finest French classical food, with great wine, great service and a comfortable atmosphere. It has to be timeless as well. Going minimal wouldn't work for us.

I learned to take criticism, but it isn't easy for a son to have the same career as his father. For a start, you argue more. I've clashed with my father over the years because I've wanted to bring in new things, new ideas to the business. But I have a good relationship with him too, and I had a wonderful childhood in the country.

The Roux scholarship

The Roux Scholarship is now in its 25th year. The judging panel is made up of my father, my uncle Michel, my cousin Alain and me, as well as Brian Turner, Heston Blumenthal, Gary Rhodes, David Nichols, Andrew Fairlie and a visiting judge. We set a theme – say mackerel – and the entrants have to send in a recipe on that. They then cook the recipes for us and we judge them blind. We don't know who is cooking. We also give them a surprise basket of ingredients to prepare a dessert. We then whittle the numbers down to six and those six have a cook-off on the finals day of a classic recipe, which we give them only an hour before.

The winner gets a financial reward and three months' work in any three-star Michelin restaurant they choose. Also, it means we give them help and advice for the rest of their professional life. It's like a family, a big family. We're always there to give them help. We also have regular meetings and outings. Last year we went to Dubai and Italy.

The scholarship is not just something you win. You're a Roux scholar for life and it's something all of us are very proud of.

FROM LEFT TO RIGHT:
my uncle Michel, me,
my father and my
cousin Alain.

OPPOSITE FROM TOP LEFT:
Silvano Giraldin. A painting
of the entrance to Le
Gavroche which we use
on our menus and cards.
Me – taking a moment
to relax for once.

When we came to live in London, it was a terrible wrench not to see so much of my father and I used to fight with my sister a lot. My father was very helpful in giving me advice on my career, and so was my uncle. Michel was the one who recommended I do the apprenticeship at Hellegouarche because he knew the circle of master pâtissiers in France.

When I came back from France and began working in the family business, it was father and son again, but we were also in a funny way working at arm's length because it was business. Now, it's much warmer and closer. My father's qualities are endless, but I'd say his most outstanding characteristics are his drive and his passion. He's a self-taught businessman and he has a fantastic business acumen that he's developed from reading books and mixing with business people. He's also very clever. You can see that when he plays poker – he can memorise everyone's cards. And I haven't even started on his cooking ability.

I think he probably admires my patience. In many ways, I do think it's harder to take over from your father than to open your own restaurant. There are different pressures and obstacles. Perhaps by taking over here, I did not have so many financial pressures, but there were huge psychological and social challenges, great barriers to push through. Even now, I still get people saying I've had it easy. But that doesn't worry me any more. I never asked for anything from my father – and he never gave me anything unless he thought I deserved it. My uncle was the same with his son, Alain. Alain had to work for eight years as a sous-chef in his father's kitchen under a head chef. He was number two for years before he got the job and he worked his balls off to get that. It was the same for me, and yet most people just don't understand that.

I haven't clashed with my uncle because I've had nothing to do with The Waterside Inn at Bray (where Michel has been since the business was split in 1987). In many ways, it was good financial housekeeping to split the business. There were so many outlets, so many different aspects of the company that it was decided my father would have Le Gavroche and my uncle The Waterside Inn.

With my father at Le Gavroche in around 1989.

There have been some rumours and stories that my father and uncle don't get on very well and haven't spoken to each other for years. That's very far from the truth. They adore each other, but there is a very strong sibling rivalry, which is absolutely normal. It's the usual love- hate relationship you get in families. They're very different people. They're brothers, not twins, but they do share the same passion for great food and wine. That brings them together as they strive for perfection.

I didn't appreciate what a massive thing I'd taken on until I did so. I didn't realise what Le Gavroche signified and how people saw my father and uncle. I suppose I didn't realise just how famous they were and how much people looked up to them. Most of the top names have been here to learn, not only the chefs like Rowley Leigh, Gordon Ramsay and Marcus Wareing, but also front-of-house staff, trained by us and Silvano Giraldin, who was with Le Gavroche for nearly 40 years until he retired in 2008.

Those first few years were tough mentally. My father found it difficult to let go, and not look at the menus. The clients were sometimes difficult, and again, people were waiting for me to fail. Some regular customers were almost disparaging, telling me that my father would do it this way, or my father's recipe was better, or I'd changed the cheese in the soufflé. In fact, nothing changed at first. Everything was still cooked in exactly the same way to the

**Me with my
uncle Michel.**

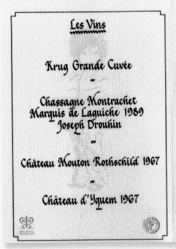

Menu from the dinner held to celebrate the 25th anniversary of Le Gavroche in 1992.

same recipes. Taking over was a huge responsibility because of the Le Gavroche name and because of its history. Le Gavroche doesn't go in and out of fashion and many of our clients have been coming here for years.

So at first I changed absolutely nothing, not for the first couple of years anyway. That's why the comments about things not being the same rankled so much. Bloody idiots. They thought they were gourmets and they couldn't even taste the cheese properly. And in fact, my father was rarely in the kitchen by the end of his time in charge, so the comments and comparisons rankled even more.

These were not the best years of Le Gavroche for me, this period of transition. I needed to stay still, to consolidate my position and so I didn't put my own ideas forward. But after a while, I began to feel more at ease with things, more at ease with myself, so I started generally lightening the whole thing – the menus and just the general atmosphere.

For example, in the early days of Le Gavroche, junior staff members were not allowed to talk to customers, but things have become more relaxed and nowadays it would appear rude not to talk to people. Gradually I started introducing more of my own style. The food was still French, still classical in the way I'd been brought up, but it evolved to my way of doing things and it's no longer stagnating.

LOBSTER WITH GARLIC BUTTER

This dish is a family favourite and one of the best ways to enjoy lobster. Simple, but delicious, it's often on the menu at Le Gavroche and can be served as a starter or a main course.

SERVES 4 AS A MAIN COURSE

250ml dry white wine

4 slices of lemon

1 tablespoon white peppercorns

3 tablespoons sea salt

4 lobsters, each 450–500g

1 bay leaf

1 sprig of thyme

GARLIC BUTTER

250g butter, room temperature

6 cloves garlic, finely chopped

1 medium shallot, finely chopped

6 tablespoons chopped parsley

salt, pepper

1 tablespoon Pernod

BÉARNAISE SAUCE

MAKES ABOUT 175ML

250g unsalted butter

2 shallots, finely chopped

3 tablespoons snipped fresh tarragon

3 tablespoons white wine vinegar or tarragon vinegar

1 teaspoon crushed white peppercorns

4 egg yolks

2 tablespoons snipped fresh chervil

Pour 4 litres of water into a large pan, add the wine, lemon, herbs, salt and peppercorns and bring to the boil. Kill the lobsters by piercing the head with a large pointed knife, then place them in the pan. Boil for 8–10 minutes, then leave to cool in the water for 10 minutes. Remove the lobsters and place on a rack for at least an hour to cool completely. Meanwhile, make the garlic butter by mixing all of the other ingredients into the soft butter.

Now remove the claws from the lobsters and crack open to collect the flesh. Split each lobster in half lengthways, remove the grit sac and intestinal track. Gently pull out the flesh without detaching the head. Smear a little garlic butter into the shell, then place the flesh back, putting the claw meat in the head cavity. Smear more garlic butter on top. Bake in a hot oven, 220°C/Gas 7, for 8–10 minutes. Put on a serving dish and spoon over more simmering garlic butter. Serve immediately with béarnaise sauce.

For the béarnaise sauce

In a small saucepan, melt the butter over low heat until it foams. Spoon off the foam and leave the butter to settle. Remove the clarified butter with a ladle, discarding the whitish residue in the bottom of the pan. Set aside.

Put the shallots into a shallow pan with the tarragon, vinegar, pepper and 1 tablespoon of water. Boil to reduce by half. Remove from the heat and leave to cool.

When cold, put the vinegar mixture in a double boiler, add the egg yolks and whisk until the yolks are light and creamy, 8–10 minutes. Do not let the mixture get too hot, otherwise the eggs will scramble.

Remove from the heat and, whisking continuously, gently pour in the clarified butter. Season to taste and add the chervil just before serving with the lobster.

MOUCLADE

Another family favourite, this is often served for lunch at Le Gavroche as a starter, but my father orders a double portion as a main course.

SERVES 4

3kg mussels
olive oil
1 onion, peeled and coarsely chopped
3 cloves garlic, crushed
1 sprig of thyme and some parsley stalks
500ml dry white wine
4 shallots, finely chopped
1 tablespoon butter
2 teaspoons mild curry powder
600ml double cream
salt, pepper

Wash and scrub the mussels. Heat a large saucepan, then add a splash of olive oil with the onion, garlic, thyme and parsley stalks. Add the mussels and white wine, cover and leave for 3 minutes. Remove the lid, shake and toss the pan to turn the mussels around. Cover and continue to cook until the mussels have opened.

Pour all the contents into a colander set over a bowl to collect the juices. Strain the juices though a fine sieve. Pick the mussels and set aside, discarding any that have not opened.

In another saucepan, sweat the finely chopped shallots with the butter. When they are soft, but with no colour, add the curry powder. Continue to cook for a further 3 minutes, then add the mussel cooking juices. Boil until reduced by half, add the cream and boil again until reduced to sauce consistency. Check the seasoning and fold in the mussels. Serve immediately – do not boil or the mussels will go rubbery. If serving as a main course, pilaf rice is the perfect accompaniment.

BAR (LOUP DE MER) AU FENOUIL EN PAPILLOTE

This is a real treat and a favourite both of the Roux family and Le Gavroche customers. My father loves it with a rich hollandaise with the addition of whipped double cream (mousseline sauce), but my preferred way to eat this fish is with a squeeze of lemon and a glass of good white wine.

SERVES 4

1 sea bass, about 1kg weight
1 medium onion
50g butter
2 large heads fennel
250ml double cream
120g button mushrooms, finely chopped
1 measure of Pernod (optional)
salt and pepper

Trim, scale and de-bone the sea bass, cutting along the back of the fish and taking care not to pierce any of the skin or flesh. Remove the guts and any remaining pin bones. Rinse the fish under gently running cold water and dry very thoroughly inside and out. Wrap the fish in a clean cloth and keep refrigerated until required.

Peel and chop the onion finely and sweat in butter for about 10 minutes – do not allow it to colour. Add the fennel, finely chopped like the onion. Season the mixture and let it cook until the fennel is soft – about 20 minutes.

Turn up the heat slightly and add the double cream. Allow this to reduce by half, then correct the seasoning. Add the finely chopped mushrooms and mix them in. Cook for a further 5 minutes. Add the Pernod, if desired. Spread the mixture on a tray, cover with a piece of buttered greaseproof paper and allow it to cool completely.

Preheat the oven to 200°C/Gas 6 Take a large sheet of greaseproof paper and brush one side with oil. Lightly season the inside of the fish with salt and place it on the oiled paper – belly-side down.

Carefully fill the belly cavity of the fish with the fennel and mushroom mixture, and then place the fish on its side. Wrap it up tightly into a parcel, twisting the ends of the paper.

Cook the fish on a baking tray in the preheated oven for about 20 minutes, turning it after 10 minutes. The fish may be opened at the table or in the kitchen where the skin may be removed on one side. Wild rice is a good accompaniment.

CRAB QUICHE

SERVES 8-10
1 medium leek
1 tablespoon butter
1 teaspoon Madras curry powder
250g fresh white crabmeat
6 egg yolks
2 eggs
200ml milk
400ml double cream
60g grated Gruyère
salt, pepper
SHORTCRUST PASTRY
(MAKES ABOUT 360G)
250g plain flour, sifted
120g butter, cold
1 teaspoon salt
1 egg
2 tablespoons water

Start by making the pastry. Put the sifted flour on a clean, cold surface and make a well. Put the diced butter, salt and egg in the middle. Using your fingertips, work all the ingredients together, gradually drawing in the flour. Once the mixture has a sandy consistency add the cold water and gently knead the pastry until smooth, but do not overwork. Make into a ball, wrap in clingfilm and rest in the fridge for 2 hours.

Roll out the pastry on a floured surface to a circle about 3mm thick and use this to line a buttered 22cm flan ring. Rest in the fridge for at least 20 minutes. Prick the pastry with a fork, line with greaseproof paper and baking beans, and then bake for

20 minutes at 200°C/Gas 6. Remove the paper and beans and return the pastry shell to the oven for another 10 minutes or until the base is cooked but not too brown in colour.

Next make the filling. Top and tail the leek, split in half lengthways and cut across into fine strips. Wash it well in cold water, then drain and dry in a cloth. Melt the butter in a wide saucepan, add the leek and gently cook until tender. Season with a little salt, pepper and the curry powder and continue to cook for another 2 or 3 minutes. Turn the leeks into a mixing bowl and leave to cool.

Preheat the oven to 200°C/Gas 6. Pick the crabmeat to remove any bones or cartilage and add to the leeks. Whisk the yolks and eggs, then add the milk and cream. Season with salt and paper and add the to the leek and crab mixture.

Pour everything into the pastry shell and gently place in the preheated oven. Bake for 15 minutes, then sprinkle the grated cheese over the top of the quiche. Cook for another 5 minutes or until golden and set. Remove from the oven and leave to cool for a short while before removing the flan ring and cutting into slices.

CANETON GAVROCHE

This duck dish dates back to Lower Sloane Street and I think it is exquisite. The secret is to have the liver topping at just the right temperature and consistency.

SERVES 2

1 free-range duck
4 duck or chicken livers
1 tablespoon duck or pork fat
1 shallot, peeled and chopped
1 sprig thyme
30g cooked foie gras
salt, pepper, brandy

Season the duck inside and out and rub salt into the skin. Heat some olive oil and brown the duck on the top of the stove. Then place it in a preheated oven, 200°C/Gas 6, for about 30 minutes by which time the breasts should be nicely pink. Remove the legs and continue to roast them until crispy and well done. Once the duck has rested, remove the breasts, trim off the skin and keep warm.

Pan fry the livers over a high heat in the smoking fat, season and add the shallot and thyme, followed by the foie gras. When the livers are rare, deglaze with a little brandy and immediately pour all the contents onto a fine drum sieve, press through using a scraper and keep warm in a saucepan. Re-heat and slice the duck breast, then pour over the smooth liver pâté. You may have to beat a little hot stock into the liver to achieve the right texture and fluidity.

Serve with glazed braised turnips and carrots and a good duck jus (see p. 305). The legs can be served afterwards warm with a little lettuce, watercress and palm heart salad.

CÔTELETTES D'AGNEAU
AU VINAIGRE D'ESTRAGON

SERVES 4

60g clarified butter
12 lamb cutlets, about 800g in all
30g butter
2 medium shallots, finely chopped
100ml dry white wine
1 tablespoon tarragon vinegar
400ml double cream
2 tablespoons chopped tarragon
salt and pepper

Heat the clarified butter in a pan, put in the lamb cutlets with a little fresh butter, too, and brown them on all sides. When the cutlets are cooked to your liking, take them out and keep them warm.

Pour off the excess fat from the pan and put in the rest of the fresh butter. Add the shallots and sweat them gently for a few minutes. Deglaze with the white wine, reduce a little, then add the vinegar. Reduce this by half, and then add the cream and chopped tarragon. Reduce by half again and correct the seasoning.

Arrange the lamb cutlets on plates, garnish with little roast potatoes, carrots and French beans. Coat the cutlets lightly with the sauce.

Cheese

I'm not particularly fond of brie-style cheeses and I don't like Somerset Brie, Epoisse, or Camembert. I'm not a fan of washed rind cheeses or creamy cheeses like Munster, Brillat-Savarin, Reblochon, and Chaumes. But I do love hard cheeses, like the French Comté and Beaufort. And I like Spanish cheeses, such as Manchego and Italian Parmesan. I love goat cheese in any shape or form – soft, fresh, even curds, all the way down to the hard little nuggets of goat cheese.

At Le Gavroche we always have a wonderful array of cheeses, but over the last few years we've brought in many British cheeses as well because there's been such a renaissance in cheese making in Great Britain. Every year since the 1970s, my father has sent a Stilton to a few of our friends in France as a Christmas present. They're great fans and very appreciative of such a great cheese.

Many small farms are making great cheeses now. Stinking Bishop from Gloucestershire is one. Blue Vinney from Dorset is another. Then there is Devon Blue and all the wonderful hard cheeses – Montgomery Cheddar is particularly good and Ticklemore is a great hard goat cheese. All these can compliment a great wine.

I feel cheese is a very important part of a meal. People tend to think cheese is fattening. They say it's not good for you and it's full of saturated fat. Yes, but it's also full of calcium and that is good for you. For someone like me, who doesn't drink much milk or eat many dairy products, it can be a valuable part of the diet. And it can be a fabulous meal on its own. A wonderful cheese, a big salad and good bread is not only a delicious meal but also a well-balanced one.

I prefer having cheese before pudding, but there are occasions when cheese after pudding works best. At a big gathering or a long winter Sunday lunch, you can just leave the cheese on the table and everyone can help themselves. As the bottle of port goes around the table you can linger and linger. Afternoon becomes evening. The conversation flows freely and that to me is a perfect time. You can't really linger over a pudding. It's not the same.

OPPOSITE: Michel checking the plâteau de fromages before lunch.

I've made subtle changes at Le Gavroche, but it's still familiar. That's where many chefs go wrong, trying to reinvent the wheel. We've got third-generation customers now, grandfathers who bring in their grandsons to taste the soufflé suissesse, which is great. Of course, there are not so many eggs in the soufflé now as there used to be and not quite so much cream, because people just don't eat like that any more. But the taste and texture of the dish are just the same as always.

There are certain dishes, such as the braised beef and seasonal game, that people know and come back for. We have a couple who fly here every year from Germany just to eat the grouse, which is always done the same way – roasted on the bone with lovely bacon on top and all the traditional accompaniments of bread sauce and roasting juices. They've been coming for 20 years. Tradition is one of the things that have made this restaurant what it is and it's important to maintain.

We're always very seasonal in the restaurant. Seasons inspire. Every chef should be inspired by the changing of the seasons – you should be longing for the first of the produce from the new season. When the first asparagus comes, for example, I get very excited and want to it to be something special.

Winter can be really long, boring and lacking in inspiration, and by the end, when there is hardly any game, you want to move away from the braised dishes and the slow-cooked recipes. And you think, 'Come on spring. Let's get going and see some sunshine and some asparagus and baby vegetables.' You just want to get in there and cook some different things. The first box of asparagus is fantastic. We get ours from Norfolk and Kent and it's served as a starter or with fish as a main course. Then the next week we might serve it as a salad with some smoked bacon. It's that change of weather and change of seasons that inspires us.

Many chefs find they cook better in some seasons than others. My preferred time is probably the end of summer and beginning of autumn, when we're just coming into the game season but there are still peaches around and other fruits such as figs.

OPPOSITE: The previous menu cover from the time when Albert was in charge at Le Gavroche.

Gavroche

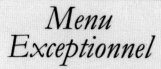

Menu
Exceptionnel

(Pour l'Ensemble de la Table)
Last order 10pm

Coquille St. Jacques "à la Coque", Parfumée au Gingembre
Scallop baked in the shell, flavoured with ginger
–◊–

Petit Soufflé Suissesse
Cheese Souffle Cooked on Double Cream
–◊–

Filet de Bar Poêlé,
Coulis de Poivrons Rôtis, Polenta, Croûtons à la Tapenade et Rouille
Seared Sea Bass on a Soft Polenta, Roasted Red Pepper Coulis,

Olive and Garlic Croutons
–◊–

Escalope de Foie Gras Chaud et Pastilla à la Cannelle
Hot Foie Gras and Crispy Pancake of Duck Flavoured with Cinnamon
–◊–

Agneau de Lait des Pyrénées Rôti,
Flageolets, Carottes et Petits Navets
Roast Lamb from The Pyrenees,
Flageolets Beans with Wild Mushrooms, Thyme Jus
–◊–

Le Plateau de Fromages
Selection of French and British Farmhouse Cheese
–◊–

Carpaccio d'Ananas au Rhum Blanc et Boule de Berlin
Fourrée de Dulce de Leche
Thin Slices of Pineapple Scented with White Rum,
Warm Doughnut Filled with Milk Caramel
–◊–

Gâteau Opéra et son Sorbet Chocolat
Bitter Chocolate and Coffee Layered Sponge Cake and Chocolate Sorbet
–◊–

Café et Petits Fours

This menu can be served with a glass of wine for each course
Selected for you by our Sommelier

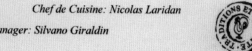

Chef Patron: Michel A. Roux   Chef de Cuisine: Nicolas Laridan

General Manager: Silvano Giraldin

Whatever the season, I do think the balance of a dish is vital. What makes a balanced dish? There is so much talk about this. To me, a balanced dish is one that hits all the right buttons. It has got the taste, the flavours and the textures, which means you get to the last mouthful and you think – gosh, I could have another mouthful. It leaves you wanting a bit more.

There are so many aspects to making a good plate of food – for example, the balance of acidity to sweetness, what the Italians call the *agrodolce*. It's very hard to define exactly, but let's take a traditional English dish of stew with dumplings. A total imbalance would be two pieces of meat and five dumplings, with loads of sauce. Or not enough sauce on the plate. You need enough sauce to moisten the meat and sufficient dumplings to mop up the sauce without dominating the dish.

Very often now, chefs will just use some dots or smears of sauce on the plate and it's not enough. If you're serving a terrine, for example, with some chutney or sauce on the side, the chef should imagine himself sitting down and taking one piece of the terrine and then a bit of the sauce. If he or she gets half way through the terrine and there's no more sauce, then it isn't balanced. It seems incredibly obvious, but too often chefs don't see it that way. They see what is on the plate as more about how it looks, rather than ingredients that people want to eat.

But you can't have steadfast rules to everything because chefs are always pushing the boundaries these days. However, to be innovative just for the sake of it is not good cooking, but just a gimmick. There are some weird and crazy ingredients in the world and to try and marry some of them with, say, fish, is not good cooking the way I see it.

Fish is such a delicate food, with such subtle flavour. I can't understand anyone wanting to mask that delicate taste. You should be looking to enhance it, not overpower it. For example, fruit and fish are difficult to pair together. It's a troublesome marriage, and very hard to get it right. Shellfish are easier, as they can work well with citrus fruits.

A Gavroche menu from about four or five years ago, featuring some of our classic dishes.

Similarly there should always be contrasting textures in food because textures play an important part in a dining experience. There should always be a creamy, a crunchy, and a soft part to every meal. Why do we like pork crackling? Because it's got a lovely crunch to it and it's all part of the sensation of eating. You can get textures into a dish in many different ways. Pork crackling is one way with a pork dish, and there are biscuits or tuiles – there are a hundred and one ways to add texture. With fish, I like a lovely crispy skin – you can either take the skin off and crisp it up separately or cook the fish with the skin on, and make it crisp by flouring it or cooking it with fresh butter.

Heston Blumenthal takes the idea of the dining experience one step further by putting iPods on people's heads when they're eating fish so they so can hear the sea and the sound of waves. Apparently it enhances the pleasure in a subliminal way. I can understand this. I wouldn't dream of doing it at Le Gavroche, but I do understand it.

It's also important to have a balanced menu and a lot of chefs don't pay attention to that. It's wonderful for a customer to sit down and look at a menu and think, 'I'd like to try this and this and that.' You want them to be enthralled and want to order lots of things, to be spoiled for choice, so they can choose something light to start and then something heavier to follow. I suppose it does come down to experience, and again chefs should put themselves in the diner's position and imagine they are eating in the restaurant.

I eat in my own restaurant every now and then for that very reason. I don't particularly like doing it, but it's important to take a customer's point of view and to really taste the food. Chefs are often accused of over seasoning and that's because when we're working we taste just a teaspoon of sauce or a tiny bit of mousse. We're not eating the whole plate of food. If you're tasting just a small amount, you can think, yes, that's a great hit of flavour. But you need to think of the person who's going to be eating a whole plate of it, and think what it's going to be like for them. Several spoons later, it might be a bit much. Also, because chefs are in a hot kitchen, they sweat a lot and so their bodies want more salt.

OPPOSITE: Morning prep time in the kitchens – cleaning fish, opening scallops, and jointing meat.

There are a lot of factors to consider. Too many chefs get very egotistical and think the customers should enjoy whatever they are cooking. OK – fair enough, but nonetheless you are in a business and you need to listen to your customers. If they think the dish is too salty or not enjoyable, then you should pay attention to that.

One of the reasons I changed the recipe for one of our signature dishes, the soufflé suissesse, is that times changed and people were not eating as much dairy produce as they used to. Half a pint of cream, 100 grams of cheese and the equivalent of four eggs became just a bit much for diners – as a starter! I love dairy foods. I couldn't live without butter and I eat it every day of the week, but in moderation. I strongly believe dairy products are good for you if they're not eaten to excess.

We tend not to follow fashion at Le Gavroche. There are a couple of fashions that are taking over the restaurant world at the moment, and I'm not too impressed with them. First, there are these bunches of tiny leaves or cress, which are wonderfully fragrant but seem to be appearing everywhere, even in top, Michelin-starred restaurants. The leaves are absolutely delicious, but I don't think there is always a place for them on top of a beautifully cooked piece of fish with a nice sauce and a vegetable garnish. You don't need cold leaves thrown all over hot food. It doesn't bring anything to the dish, but it's in, it's fashionable.

Something else which is overdone right now is foam. Ferran Adrià of El Bulli in Gerona, Spain, pioneered it and he does it very well. I've tried several of his foams and they are good. But there's no crunch, there is no texture... there is nothing there except air. It can be flavoursome air, which is great, but why go to all the trouble to purée something that starts off as a good ingredient, then add gelatine to it in some form, pump it up with gas and siphon it onto a plate? It's not for me. I don't want to cook like that and I don't enjoy eating like that. And the only way to make a foam last from the kitchen to the table is to put so much gelling agent in it, or lecithin, that it's not natural and it's not right. You'll never find a soda siphon in my kitchen. I think it's just a gimmick.

Hot jellies are another gimmick of fashion. Why make jellies hot? Why serve a jelly on hot food? I can't get my head around it. Recently I saw a red wine sauce with red wine jelly. So they've made a red wine reduction, then they've added a gelling agent, put it in a syringe and put little droplets into a chemical solution to set them. Then you have to drain and wash them because you don't want people to be eating the chemicals, and serve them in the sauce. These jellies don't melt in warm temperatures, but why? What are we eating? It is bizarre and it can't be good for you. If it's not melting at blood temperature, then it is completely unnatural. And I don't think it gives any extra flavour to the dish. Far better to provide a good sauce and leave the syringes out of the kitchen.

When I was judging the professional MasterChef series recently, it was absolutely fascinating to see what people brought into the kitchens – things that have nothing to do with the preparation of good food. Journalists can get carried away with these kinds of wizardry and eulogise about them, but without real knowledge of gastronomy and what goes into good food. Times change and what was once perceived as the best can soon become passé. Inspectors and journalists are brought up on fads and fantasies so their view of fine dining is a specific one, and that's why places such as Le Gavroche and other great restaurants are no longer considered worthy of three stars. There is an element of fashion in any restaurant award.

Heston Blumenthal and some others are very clever and brilliant at what they do, but there are hundreds of other chefs who try these complex things, even though they don't really understand what they're doing. That is not only scary but dangerous. If you ask Heston what his favourite dish is, he'll tell you it is roast chicken. Ferran Adrià is the same. His favourite restaurant is a local café serving grilled sardines. For me, it would be the same – something simple. You just cannot beat real tastes and good food.

For the professional MasterChef series, three finalists cooked for five top restaurateurs and the winning main course was roast chicken, creamy mashed potatoes, wild mushrooms and creamed leeks. How do you impress restaurateurs – the owner of Nobu, the owner of Sketch, the owner of Pied à Terre? Do you impress them with foams and jellies or food with little dots and smears all over the plate? No! In my view, it's far more difficult to roast a piece of meat properly than to make a mousse or jelly, because to make a mousse or jelly, you just need to follow a recipe and then perhaps use a ruler to cut it into slices. Anyone off the street could be taught to do that. It's far harder to teach someone how to roast a piece of meat to perfection. We're losing the fundamental skills of fine cuisine. A good chef can tell if meat is cooked by touch, even just by the look of it. There is far more skill in that than people think. It all harks back to home cooking – haute cuisine comfort food. That is the kind of food we serve here at Le Gavroche.

A perfectly cooked roast chicken, with wonderful crispy skin, perfect morel mushrooms, and good creamy mash – that to me is gastronomy. That to me is good food to enjoy with a fine wine.

What really annoys me are things like a trio of chicken or a trio of lamb, all cooked in different ways. The other night here we served a rack of lamb and also some slices of leg. That's about as sophisticated as it will get at Le Gavroche. And the proof is there – simple food is what most leading chefs like to eat. You just cannot beat properly cooked food, made with good ingredients.

Of course, you change with the times. At Le Gavroche we've lightened up a lot and not just with the food. There was a time here when the waiters were not allowed to speak to the clients. Only the maitre d' or the manager would talk to the clients. The waiters just brought the food and stood to attention. That has changed. Now the waiters are encouraged to talk, to be friendly and to smile. Men no longer need to wear a tie, although most do. Still, men have to wear jackets. And no trainers or torn jeans, definitely not for dinner. At lunchtime you can have a bit more latitude. And we do have shirts and jackets available if people want them. Le Gavroche is formal dining and we wouldn't want it any other way.

LAGER AND LIME SORBET

This is a refreshing sorbet which can be served
at the beginning or end of a meal.

SERVES 8
880ml premium lager
juice and zest of 2 limes
2 tablespoons lime cordial
500ml sugar syrup
1 tablespoon ice cream stabiliser (optional)

To make the sugar syrup, add 500g caster sugar to 400ml water
and bring to the boil. Leave to chill.

Mix the lager, lime juice and zest, cordial, syrup and stabiliser
together. Freeze in an ice cream machine or place in a bowl in
the freezer. After a couple of hours whisk the mixture well and
return to the freezer. Continue whisking and freezing until
smooth and set. Serve in little cocktail glasses.

COEUR D'ARTICHAUT LUCULLUS
STUFFED ARTICHOKE WITH FOIE GRAS AND TRUFFLES

This was one of the first dishes I brought to Le Gavroche. It is the quintessence of what Le Gavroche is about – luxury and extravagance, taste and texture, and a lot of time and skill.

SERVES 4

4 globe artichokes
lemon
1 large chicken breast (about 225g), skinned
1 egg white
300ml double cream
4 teaspoons truffle paste
120g foie gras, cut into cubes and seared but still pink
1 medium truffle, cooked
salt, white pepper

Trim the artichokes of all their leaves, then cook in boiling, salted water with a generous squeeze of lemon. They should take about 15 minutes. When tender, leave to cool in the liquid. With the help of a spoon, remove the choke (the stringy inedible centre) and trim each artichoke to a perfect circle.

Place the chicken breast and egg white in a food processor and blitz until puréed. Press through a fine sieve. Place in a bowl over ice and slowly beat in the cream, season with salt and little white pepper.

In the centre of each artichoke, place a little truffle paste followed by some foie gras. With a dessertspoon, cover with the chicken mousse. Shape this into an even sphere, making sure the foie gras does not show. Decorate with the truffle slices. Gently, but tightly, wrap in clingfilm and cook in a steamer for 15 minutes. Serve with a sweet Madeira sauce (see p. 306).

SPICY OCTOPUS SALAD

This requires quite a bit of preparation and work beforehand, but it's actually simple and well worth the time. If possible, buy frozen octopus as it will always be more tender than fresh. Alternatively, freeze the octopus yourself, then defrost when you need it.

SERVES ABOUT 12

1 octopus, about 1kg
1 sprig of thyme
1 bay leaf
2 slices of lemon
1 tablespoon black peppercorns
sea salt

TOMATO DRESSING
6 tomatoes, red and yellow
1 red chilli
2 spring onions, thinly sliced
juice of 1 lime
1 tablespoon cane sugar syrup
2 tablespoons olive oil
salt, fresh coriander

Wash the octopus under cold water. Make sure it has been gutted and the beak removed. Cover with cold water, add the herbs, lemon, peppercorns and a generous amount of sea salt. Bring to a gentle simmer and cook for about 2½ hours or until tender. Leave to cool completely in the water.

Drain the octopus and carefully place on a double layer of clingfilm. Roll this into a sausage about 3cm wide. Secure the ends and place in the freezer to set. You can now take it out to use as and when needed. Just let it thaw a little and slice as thinly as possible with a sharp, thin-bladed knife. Arrange the slices in one layer on a plate and serve with the tomato dressing.

For the tomato dressing
Skin, deseed and dice the tomatoes. Add the thinly sliced chilli with or without seeds, depending on how spicy you want the salad to be, along with the spring onions. Season and add the lime juice, syrup, olive oil, seasoning and finally the shredded coriander.

HOT FOIE GRAS WITH DUCK PASTILLA AND CINNAMON

If you can't find brique pastry (North African paper-thin pancakes), you can use spring roll pastry for this dish.

SERVES 4

2 duck legs confit (see p. 185)
1 dessertspoon soy sauce
1 dessertspoon Hoisin sauce
4 sheets of brique pastry (pastilla pancakes)
1 egg, beaten
oil for cooking
paprika, ground cinnamon, icing sugar
4 slices duck foie gras, 80g each
750ml strong red wine
100ml port
2 dessertspoons caster sugar
5 cinnamon sticks
50g butter
salt, pepper

Shred the duck meat and mix in the soy and Hoisin sauce. Divide this between the 4 sheets of pastry and shape into neat parcels, 6 x 3cm. Seal the edges with a little beaten egg and cut away any excess. Deep fry in the oil until crisp, then dust with paprika, cinnamon and icing sugar. Pan fry the foie gras in a hot, dry pan until golden on both sides, then turn down the heat to continue to cook gently. The foie gras should be soft yet a little bouncy to the touch.

For the sauce, rapidly boil the wine and port with the sugar and cinnamon until reduced to 100ml. Strain, then bring to the boil again. Whisk in the butter and check for seasoning. The sauce may need a little more sugar, depending on the wine. Drizzle the sauce onto the plate and cut the pastilla diagonally. Serve with the foie gras.

SPICY AUBERGINE SALAD WITH COCONUT

This dish is adapted from a Sri Lankan recipe that a young chef in the kitchens of Le Gavroche cooked for me. We serve it in the restaurant for little 'amuse-bouche' topped with a grilled prawn, but at home I make a big bowl to serve with any kind of grilled seafood. It is so good it can also be eaten on its own as a delicious summer salad.

SERVES 6

4 large aubergines
vegetable oil for frying
salt, chilli powder
2 tablespoons tomato ketchup
1 tablespoon wholegrain Dijon mustard
juice of 1 lemon
2 spring onions, thinly sliced
50g coconut chips, toasted

Trim off the ends of the aubergines. Cut lengthways into slices about 15mm thick, then into cubes. Heat up a large, non-stick pan with a generous amount of vegetable oil. When the oil is smoking hot, put in the aubergine cubes. They will soak up all the oil, but don't worry – carry on cooking over high heat until the aubergine is lightly browned, then turn down the heat to gently simmer until tender. The whole cooking process should take about 12 minutes.

Season well with salt and chilli powder to taste. Remember, if the salad is to be served cold it will need more seasoning than if eaten warm. Put the aubergines in a colander to drain and leave for about 10 minutes for some of the oil to seep out. Return the aubergine to the pan and over low heat, fold in the ketchup, mustard and lemon juice. Simmer for 3–4 minutes, then remove and chill. Just before serving, fold in the spring onions and toasted coconut crisps.

LOBSTER MANGO SALAD

SERVES 4

   2 cooked lobsters, 500–600g each
   1 avocado, ripe but firm
   1 mango, ripe but firm
   2 spring onions, sliced
   juice of 2 limes
   peel of 1 lime, cut into thin strips
      and cooked in a sugar syrup
   12 basil leaves
   4 tablespoons extra virgin olive oil
   salt
   green Tabasco
   endive leaves for serving (optional)

Cut the lobster tail meat into medallions and all the rest into dice.
Peel the avocado and mango and dice the flesh. Add the spring
onions, lime juice and peel, torn basil leaves, olive oil and seasoning.
Toss very gently.

Serve the salad in glass bowls or spoon into little endive leaves.

CHICKEN WITH HONEY AND ROSEMARY BAKED IN A SALT CRUST

SERVES 4 TO 6

SALT CRUST
1kg plain flour
2 egg whites
3 tablespoons chopped rosemary
450ml water
250g fine table salt
400g coarse sea salt

CHICKEN
1 good-quality chicken, about 2.2kg
2 tablespoons clear honey
good pinch paprika
pepper

4 chicken livers
100g mixed dry mushrooms, soaked overnight
2 tablespoons butter
6 pure meat pork sausages, skins removed
2 tablespoons fresh breadcrumbs
1 bunch chives, chopped
1 egg
2 sprigs rosemary

Brush the chicken with the honey mixed with paprika and pepper. This is best done the day before and repeated 2 or 3 times. Keep in the refrigerator. To make the salt crust, mix the flour, egg whites and chopped rosemary with the water to form a paste. Add both kinds of salt and knead well for 5 minutes. Wrap in clingfilm and refrigerate.

Cut the livers into large dice. Drain, rinse and chop the mushrooms and cook them in the foaming butter for 5–6 minutes. Add the livers and continue to cook and stir for 2–3 minutes. When cool, add the sausage meat and mix well with a fork. Then add the breadcrumbs, chives and egg.

When you're ready to cook the chicken, roll out the salt dough and place 2 sprigs of rosemary in the place where the chicken will be. Stuff the chicken, then cover the bird completely with dough, making sure there are no air pockets and it is completely sealed. Bake in a preheated oven at 200°C/Gas 6 for 50 minutes, then leave to rest out of the oven for 15 minutes before breaking open the crust.

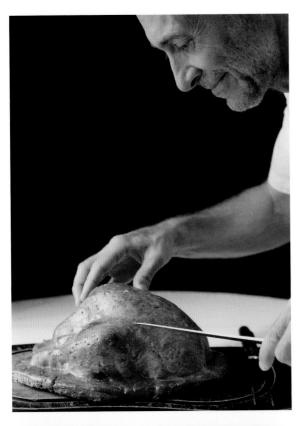

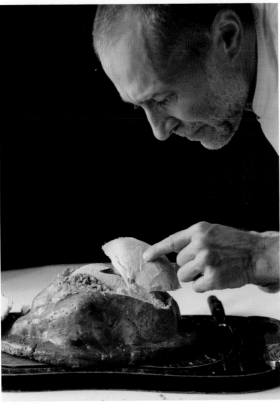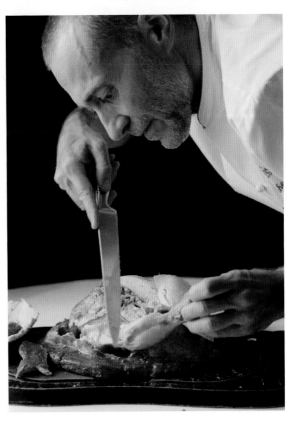

QUEUE DE BOEUF FARCIE ET BRAISÉE

SERVES 8

2 oxtails, 1.5kg each
    including bones
1 splash of brandy
caul fat (crepinette) to make
    a sheet 30 x 30 cm
160g raw foie gras (optional)
2 onions
1 carrot
2 sticks of celery
2 cloves garlic, peeled
butter and oil
1 bottle full-bodied red wine
250ml port
1 bouquet garni
100g smoked bacon, diced
1 litre veal stock (see p. 303)
salt and pepper

STUFFING
60g smoked bacon
200g lean pork (fillet)
100g pork belly, fatty
100g pork fat
1 sprig of thyme
salt, pepper and nutmeg

Trim some of the excess fat from the thick end of the oxtail. Chop off the thinnest part so you are left with a length of 25cm. Turn the oxtail upside down so the smooth side is on the work surface and, using a sharp boning knife, follow the bone structure from one end to the other removing the bone. This is a tricky job so go slowly and take care not to make too many holes. The end result should look like an oblong carpet, not a string vest! If you have a helpful local butcher you might be able to get him to bone the oxtails for you.

Keep the bones and the thin part of the tail for braising. Season the tail meat and douse with brandy. Then cover with clingfilm and refrigerate for an hour.

Meanwhile make the stuffing. Remove the rind from the smoked bacon and dice all the meat and fat. Put it through a mincer with a medium-size (4mm) disc. Pick the leaves off the thyme and mix into the stuffing with the seasoning. Beat well and then bake a spoonful of the mix in a foil wrapper to check the seasoning.

Rinse the caul fat and lay it flat on a clean work surface. Put an oxtail, skin-side down, on the centre of the caul. Make the stuffing into a sausage shape and place it on the oxtail. If using foie gras, make it into a long strip, 1cm thick, to go the length of the oxtail and place onto the stuffing. Put the other oxtail on top, then roll the caul fat tightly round everything. Using butchers' string, tie lengthways and across at equal intervals to make a neat, tight sausage. Cut the vegetables into 3cm cubes.

In a wide pan big enough to take the oxtail, lightly brown it in butter and oil. Remove the oxtail and add the bones, cubed vegetables and garlic. When these are well caramelised, add the wine, port, bouquet garni, salt, pepper and smoked bacon. Bring to the boil, add the oxtail and veal stock and bring to the boil again. Skim, then simmer partially covered for 2½ hours until the meat is tender to touch. Leave to cool in this liquid. When the oxtail is cool enough to handle, take it out and gently remove the strings. Roll tightly in clingfilm to make a perfect sausage shape and chill in the refrigerator overnight.

Pass the sauce through a fine sieve and then reduce over high heat until sauce consistency. Skim all the fat that comes to the top. Finish the sauce with a little butter to give it shine and a velvety finish.

Cut 3cm slices of oxtail, put them on a plate, cover with clingfilm and steam to reheat. Serve with the sauce and mashed potato (see p. 159).

MAGRET DE CANARD
À LA BORDELAISE

SERVES 4

2 large duck breasts (magrets)
400g shallots
2 bottles of red wine
2 litres veal stock (see p. 303)
1 bouquet garni
100g butter
flat-leaf parsley
salt, pepper
2 pieces of bone marrow, soaked
   in cold water for two hours

Trim most of the fat off the duck breasts, leaving a thin layer of about 3mm, and remove all the sinew from the other side. Prick 12 times with a fork.

Peel the shallots, slice into thin rounds and put them in a deep-sided, thick-bottomed pan with the red wine. Place the pan on a moderate heat and allow the wine to reduce slowly, until it is one-eighth of its original volume. Add the veal stock, a pinch of salt and the bouquet garni and cook very slowly, preferably in a low oven at 140°C/Gas 1 for about 2½ hours.

Preheat a pan and add the seasoned duck breasts, fatty side down. Enough fat will come out of the magrets in which to cook them. Cook the breasts until they are golden brown on both sides and a nice pink colour inside – 'rose' as we say. This will take about 15 minutes. Remove them from the pan and keep hot.

Having pre-soaked the marrow in cold water, drain it and cut into 2cm thick slices. Poach the slices gently in simmering, salted water, until they are a creamy white colour, which should take 1 or 2 minutes. Drain the marrow well on a piece of kitchen paper.

Remove the shallots from the oven, take out the bouquet garni. Check for seasoning and whisk in the butter, cut in little pieces. Carve the magrets into long thin slices and arrange the marrow on top. Serve the shallots separately.

To accompany this dish, I would recommend a nice endives meunière and/or a gratin dauphinois (see p. 181) with some mangetout.

ENDIVES MEUNIÈRE

SERVES 4
4 endives
1 tablespoon butter
salt, pepper
pinch of sugar
1 lemon

Blanch the endives in salted, boiling water for 5 minutes. Remove and refresh in iced water. Drain and gently press in paper towel to dry.

Then cut the endives in half lengthways and pan fry in butter until golden brown. Season with salt, pepper and a pinch of sugar, then add a squeeze of lemon juice.

ROAST SADDLE OF RABBIT
WITH ALE SAUCE AND LEEKS

2 large leeks, trimmed and washed
oil and butter for cooking
4 saddles of rabbit
1 medium onion, peeled and sliced
100ml good brown ale
1 tablespoon lemon juice
1 tablespoon treacle
200ml chicken stock (see p. 304)
salt, pepper

First blanch the leeks in salted, boiling water until tender, then refresh in iced water. Drain and slice into rounds about 1cm thick.

Preheat the oven to 200°C/Gas 6. Heat a little oil in a cast-iron casserole dish and brown the seasoned rabbit until golden on all sides. Add a little butter and the onion, then place in the oven for 15 minutes. Remove the rabbit from the casserole and leave to rest in a warm place.

Put the casserole dish back on the stove and pour in the ale, lemon juice and treacle. Boil until almost dry, then add the stock and simmer for 10 minutes. Whisk a tablespoon of butter into the sauce, then pass through a fine sieve.

Pan fry the leeks in a non-stick pan with a little oil and butter until brown. Remove the loins from the saddles and place on top of the leeks. Serve with the sauce and some gnocchi or roast potatoes.

ROASTED PEACHES WITH PISTACHIOS

4 large white peaches
1 tablespoon butter
4 tablespoons castor sugar
juice of 1 lemon
4 tablespoons sweet wine
60g pistachios peeled

To peel the peaches, place them in boiling water for 20 seconds, then lift out and plunge into iced water to stop the cooking. Drain well and carefully peel off the skin.

Preheat the oven to 180°C/Gas 4. Heat an ovenproof, non-stick roasting pan on top of the stove. Add the butter and when it's foaming, put in the peaches, navel-side up. When browned turn over and sprinkle with the sugar.

Put the peaches into the oven and bake for 5 minutes, then baste with the cooking juices. Carry on cooking until the peaches are tender, about 15 minutes, basting regularly. Remove the peaches from the roasting pan and keep warm.

Put the pan back on to the stove and pour in the lemon juice and wine. Boil for 2 to 3 minutes, then add the pistachios. Pour this onto the peaches and serve hot.

COCONUT PANNA COTTA

You do need proper coconut purée for this recipe, not coconut cream or milk. Coconut purée is pure coconut flesh that has been puréed and put through a fine sieve. Some Asian stores stock frozen purée, or you could try making your own with fresh coconut. It must be very finely sieved to achieve the fine texture. We get our coconut purée from Les Vergers Boiron (www.boironfreres.com).

SERVES 8

600g coconut purée
2 sheets gelatine, soaked
100g white chocolate
2 tablespoons Malibu

Soak the gelatine in cold water and then squeeze. Gently heat the coconut until very hot, then whisk in the soaked gelatine. Pour this onto the melted chocolate, mix well then add the Malibu. Pass through a fine sieve and pour into individual moulds to set overnight. Serve with some diced mango and coconut crisps.

FLOATING ISLANDS WITH STRAWBERRY COMPOTE

The floating island without the strawberries is an Easter traditional dessert in France. But I love it anytime of the year and with strawberry compote, it is so good that it has become a summer-time favourite of Le Gavroche clients.

SERVES 4

500g strawberries
100g sugar or to taste
6 egg whites
340g caster sugar
300g caster sugar for caramel and poaching liquid
crème Anglaise (see p. 308)

To make the strawberry compote, simply sprinkle a little sugar over some washed and hulled strawberries. The amount of sugar depends on the sweetness of the berries. Bring this to the boil, then immediately take off the heat, cover and leave to cool.

Beat the egg whites with a whisk until frothy, then add 340g caster sugar. Continue to whisk until firm and smooth. Using a big kitchen spoon dipped in cold water, scoop out a big island of meringue and plunge the spoon into simmering sweetened water. The island should come off the spoon and poach in this liquid. Carry on doing this until all the egg whites are used, not forgetting to flip the islands over after 3–4 minutes to cook on both sides. Once cooked, gently take the islands out of the liquid with a slotted spoon. Place on a rack to cool and drain. When cold, pour over the top some freshly made caramel – simply heat some sugar in a heavy pan until liquid and golden.

To serve, place some compote in each bowl, followed by crème Anglaise flavoured with vanilla, and finally the caramel-coated floating islands.

I run a tightly organised kitchen. I can't work any other way and staff don't last here very long if they work in a mess. I'm very insistent that there is a right way and a wrong way to do things. It's all about being methodical and ergonomic. That's been drummed into me right from the first days of my apprenticeship. I learned so much from that – the discipline and the way you approach tasks, the way you set out your workbench. And of course the way you set out your workbench depends on what task you're doing. It's simple things that should be automatic – like always putting something under your chopping board so it doesn't slip. You get out your knives that you want for the particular task, all the equipment you need so you don't have to run around looking for things. And have a list. Work to a list. All my chefs work to a list. Prioritise and break up the morning's work and organise it into categories. You can't just run around like a bull in a china shop.

I can't stand a dirty kitchen. I'm constantly ranting at the staff to keep things clean. If they drop something, they should pick it up immediately. In some kitchens, the floors are in an abysmal state – dangerous even.

We had a big clash with Westminster Council back in the late 1980s. A health inspector came in and he was particularly officious. Maybe the head chef at the time didn't pander to him enough and was a bit abrupt. But this particular inspector had issue with one cracked electric socket and found three flies in the kitchen – each fly was numbered. Things escalated and got very bad. They were threatening us with various writs and it ended up in court, costing us a lot of money. It was in the national newspapers – Le Gavroche kitchen dirty and so on, but it was totally untrue.

We hired a top QC. We even had the QCs and judge visit the kitchen to inspect it. This lasted the best part of six months and it was front page news when it was thrown out of court and we were awarded costs. One of the things my father said in court was our kitchen was so clean you could eat off the floor. And a reporter from *The Sun* came in and ate his lunch off the kitchen floor. At Le Gavroche we've always been sticklers for cleanliness. I think

it's a very important part of gastronomy and top-end cuisine that the kitchen is run very cleanly.

I hate waste. It's something we're always wary of. The majority of restaurants that aren't achieving their margins are failing because of waste. Look in their dustbins. Do they use the tops of the leeks? You certainly don't put them in the bin. You can use them in stocks and soups and sauces, or staff food. Peelings and scraps of meat are always recycled and re-used. For example, when you peel your potato and cut it into a fondant shape, you don't just throw away the rest of the potato. It can be used for mash. Potato peelings can be fried and eaten like French fries. We have them here for staff lunch. They're wonderful – crunchy and tasty.

When you peel oranges, the skins don't have to be thrown away. Cook the peel in sugar and you've got yourself a petit four. The sugar you've been rolling the orange in will taste of orange, so use that to make your next sugar syrup.

We get all our meat on the bone. We butcher everything ourselves. All the bones are used in stocks, or staff food. You can get a lot of meat off the breasts of baby lamb, for example, and that can make a delicious casserole. Pork fat we use for pâtés and mousses. Pork skin we use boiled up in sauces and ragouts. It's delicious but you have to cook it properly. It is a question of knowledge as well. It's a case of going back in time. Our grandmothers would never dream of throwing anything away. It's all part of the tradition of *maison bourgeoise* – good housekeeping – and that's something which has been lost. But perhaps that will come back as people become more aware. When we have a roast chicken at home, for example, we fight over the carcass – the parson's nose, everything. Then the carcass is used for stock.

You often see chefs wasting huge quantities of fish. You watch them filleting salmon and they end up with beautiful, perfect rectangles and then bin the trimmings. It's criminal. There is so much meat on the bones. You just get a spoon and scrape it down and use it. The belly of salmon is delicious for rillettes and the cavity behind the head holds a massive amount of meat. Think of fishcakes, mousses, terrines – everything can be used. Young chefs come in here and they fillet away and just chuck it in the bin. So I get the head, the bones, the trimmings and make them weigh the end product. If you end up with more trimmings than end product, then there is a big problem. Some of them look at me as if I'm a Martian. If they can't come round to my way of thinking I wish them luck and a prosperous career elsewhere, which I know they won't have if they continue to waste food.

We'd never throw away lobster shells or langoustine heads. In the city, when we were running Le Gamin, we'd use the lobster tail and meat, then the lobster head would be made into a bisque. When that was done, the shells would be crushed and cooked again with tomato to make a lobster butter or oil. It was a lot of work but you'd get a good return out of a lobster.

If I'm preparing a fillet of beef, which is incredibly expensive, I like to use everything so there's no waste. I tell young chefs that tournedos don't have to be a perfect circle. I've seen commis chefs cut 250 grams of fillet and shave bits off to get a perfect circle weighing 180 grams. And all the bits left over — where do they go? Again, I tell them get the scales out, weigh the trimmings and weigh the end product. This is important to me and while some of the young staff acknowledge what I'm trying to say, others just don't get it.

At Le Gavroche we never even throw away the butter wrappers. We use them for anything we'd use foil or greaseproof paper for. They're already buttered after all! And we re-use the foil too, if it hasn't been in contact with food. We soak the silver cutlery overnight in a soda solution and used aluminium foil. The two react with the silver and remove the tarnish.

And like most restaurants we use vinegar as a degreaser – it's cheaper and more effective than industrial cleaners. We never throw away our old tablecloths and napkins. Once they're no longer any good for the tables they're cut up and used as cleaning cloths.

To clean silver

1 sheet aluminium foil, about 20 x 30cm
2 litres water
2 tablespoons bicarbonate of soda

We re-use aluminium foil here, if it hasn't been in contact with food. We soak the silver cutlery overnight in a soda solution and used aluminium foil. The two react together and remove the tarnish, getting into all the little crevices.

Simply place the foil in the bottom of a plastic bucket, add water and bicarbonate of soda to cover the silver. Next morning, remove the silver, and wash and dry thoroughly.

Another thing that's important for a chef is a good palate. What makes a good palate? First of all, you're born with it, and if you're born with this ability to taste you're halfway there and you can train your palate. The sooner your children get involved in the kitchen the better. It's so important to teach children what food tastes like – a raw, ripe tomato, a French bean, even the taste of natural yoghurt are a great way to start.

If you've got a good memory, you can remember tastes and smells. But some people have an absolutely zero sense of taste and smell. The two senses are very closely related. There are certain things which when you put them into your mouth it's the smell you experience more than the taste.

At home, if my mother cooked something, my father would always pass comment. They wouldn't argue, but they'd discuss it. Invariably, my father would say at the end of the day that my mother was right. Because deep down, my father knows my mother has the finer taste buds. She has an immensely refined palate and nose. So does my daughter Emily. She has an excellent palate, probably better than mine, and she's got very finely tuned senses. We've always had fun with that, making a game of trying to guess ingredients in different dishes – that's a great way to get children interested in taste.

Unfortunately, some chefs don't have a good palate and as hard as they try, they can never get it quite right. You can teach them and they can learn a lot, but it's just that final bit of finesse – you're born with it.

Wine is the classic way of educating the palate because you're putting wine in your mouth, but you're smelling it at the back of your throat before you can taste it. I'd rather go without wine than drink something that's not good. This may sound snobbish, but it is not meant in that way at all. And you don't have to spend a fortune to drink good wine. That is a misconception. In England there is a drinking culture which goes against the appreciation of good wine, because people are more interested in the alcohol. There is an underlying culture of just boozing, which is a shame. Wine sales are going up, but it's cheap wine and not particularly good.

However, many of the finest Masters of Wine and sommeliers are British, and much of the claret region has been British owned at one time or another. And remember that up until quite recently, a lot of clarets were brought here in barrels and then bottled.

You don't have to be a wine snob, but it is fun to learn a bit about wine and anyone can do it. I strongly believe that. Anyone can differentiate a wooded Chardonnay from a Sauvignon Blanc. It's just taking the time and breaking the barriers. You may feel a bit silly at first, having a sniff instead of just quaffing your wine, but people should try to recognise the smell.

A glass of wine with a meal enhances the food and the whole sense of occasion. Most restaurants these days serve wine by the glass and good wine at that. So people shouldn't feel they have to buy a whole bottle of wine. I'm not totally rigid about the traditional thing of white wine with fish, and red wine with beef or lamb. I think you have to respect personal preferences. If people prefer red wine, then why not have it with fish? But don't choose a big heavy Shiraz or a claret. Go for something much lighter like a Pinot Noir or something from the Loire Valley. Or a rosé. There is nothing wrong with a rosé. Of course, if the fish is cooked with something a bit heavier, like a red wine sauce, then you can go for a slightly heavier wine.

However, there are certain combinations that we know do or don't work. For example, there is no way you could drink red wine with oysters. It just doesn't work. You could get away with a lightly oaked, aged chardonnay with a steak. That would be fine. Sweet wines can go well with certain cheeses. A pungent blue cheese with a white sweet wine can work as well as port or red wine. It's all about enjoyment really. Try it out, but keep it simple.

Also, don't forget that the shape of the wine glass is very important. A lot of the tasting is done through the nose, even when you're swallowing because what you're tasting is what you're smelling as well. A good wine glass releases the smell of the wine and that enhances its taste.

OPPOSITE: A wall of labels in the Gavroche wine cellar.

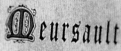

Gavroche hierarchy

BOSS!

KITCHEN

Head chef
Overall responsibility for food quality, management, hiring and firing of kitchen staff, food costs and menu development.

Sous-chef
Capable of all duties in the kitchen; link from head chef to the rest of the team. Needs seven years of working and cooking experience.

Chef de partie
Runs and organises a section (i.e. fish, meat) and responsible for cooking to the standard required and for teaching other minor chefs their tasks. Usually needs a minimum of five years working experience.

Demi-chef de partie
Has the ability to cook at the required level but needs more experience to take on the responsibility.

1st commis
A major step on the ladder. Can be left to cook and present food.

Commis
Mostly preparation. Nothing cooked or prepared will go unchecked, a workhorse.

Apprentice
The first step. A traditional apprenticeship with a good head chef as a mentor is unbeatable. Two or three years of hard graft – expect the jobs no one wants.

Kitchen porter
Without the porter the kitchen just doesn't run well. Good cooking starts with a clean pan.

FRONT OF HOUSE

General manager
Responsible for all front of house, staff management, health and safety, customer relations, reservations, recruitment. Needs two languages at least.

Assistant manager
Cover for manager, specific responsibilities given for laundry, cleaning, crockery, stocks, etc, and for staff rotas.

Maître d'hôtel
In charge of a 'carré' or a section of the dining room, with two or three more junior staff. Takes orders from customers, capable of carving, controls speed of service. Needs presence and strong character.

Chef de rang
Can take orders from clients and expected to take responsibility. Has all the skills but needs more customer relations experience to take the next step.

Demi chef de rang
Too young to become chef de rang. Needs the experience that brings the confidence needed for assurance.

Commis de salle
A lot of polishing, laying tables, cleaning and basic work. Vital that it's done properly.

Busboy
Carries out the important but menial task of delivering trays of food to the right table. Usually not looking at making a career out of waiting.

Plate/glass washer
Like the kitchen porter, vitally important. A good one saves you money from fewer breakages and makes sure everything is spotless.

A day in the life of le Gavroche

8am:

The streets of London's Mayfair are deserted. The rich sleep later than the rest of the world, and Mayfair is richer than most places. Along Upper Brook Street, curtains are still tightly drawn. It will be hours before the pavements echo to the click of expensive stilettos and the purr of waiting limousines.

But stop for a minute outside the elegant wrought-iron portico of number 43 and listen. From below in the basement comes a faint but audible hum of people at work.

And under the rising hum wafts a mouth-watering aroma of food cooking, savoury and sweet mixed together.

For the 22 kitchen staff of Le Gavroche, the day's work has already begun. Along the workbenches against the walls of this vast, subterranean kitchen, people are chopping, dicing and slicing piles of vegetables into perfect cubes, batons and circles. In the pastry area, just off the main kitchen, two cooks slide delicate puff pastry sheets into the oven, the first of many intricate preparations for pear mille-feuilles.

Trays of freshly baked petits fours are cooling on the racks, ready to be arranged on their specially designed glass plates.

In the centre of the kitchen stands a vast Rorgue range, the ultimate piece of restaurant equipment. It is bigger than a billiard table, weighs more than two and a half tonnes and cost more than £70,000. This is where the best French food in London has been cooked week after week since 1967, when Michel Jr's father, Albert, and his uncle Michel moved from their first premises across Hyde Park in Lower Sloane Street.

Most of England's top chefs began here. They learned to brown, roast, grill and sauté on these blazing gas hotplates, salamanders and ovens. Marcus Wareing from Petrus, Gordon Ramsay, Rowley Leigh from Le Café Anglais, and Pierre Koffmann from La Tante Claire... the list goes on and on.

CLOCKWISE FROM TOP LEFT: An apprentice peeling shallots. Chef lends a hand. A chef de partie in the fish kitchen. A sous-chef hard at work.

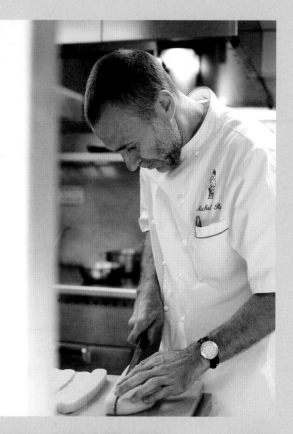

9am:

Michel Jr is on the telephone in his office, a shoebox-sized cubicle with just enough room for a desk, telephone and chair. The shelves behind him are stuffed with files of menus and recipes. As he drinks one of his many cups of strong black coffee in his favourite Manchester United mug, he checks the day's menus while keeping an accurate tally of the restaurant supplies.

His weekly grocery list includes 1,280 eggs, 60 kilos of butter, 200 kilos of potatoes in five different varieties, 80 lobsters and 500 scallops, not to mention a £4,000 order of fruit and vegetables and 30 loaves of speciality bread. Then there are the special orders, all the seasonal delicacies which change from week to week throughout the year: the first delicate wild garlic leaves, picked in Wales before their flavour becomes too bitter and pungent, French milk-fed lamb, rose-pink veal chops, wild sea bass and the first and the best of British game.

With his larder in order, Michel Jr is up and out into the main kitchen. 'Make sure they don't burn,' he says to a sous-chef who's grilling a tray of bright red peppers as he walks past. 'Half a dozen more eggs,' he directs the team making a delicate spinach mousse, 'and a touch more salt.' He walks through to the fish kitchen, where another team is carving great long loins of sea bass with surgical precision, and two French apprentices are prising fat scallops from their shells. Then it's back to his office, on the way checking the red peppers, which are now off the grill and cooling before being made into a coulis to serve with the sea bass.

Michel in his office, on the phone to suppliers while still keeping a beady eye on what's going on in the kitchen.

10am:

Everyone is working just that bit faster now. The restaurant is completely full for lunch and a company has booked the entire restaurant that evening for a private function.

Upstairs, the outside steps are scrubbed and swept and the potted plants lining the portico are watered. Any limp or brown leaves and flowers are swiftly pruned and the clippings swept away. Both the lobby and lounge have been vacuumed and dusted. The cushions are plumped up, the sofas are brushed and the glass doors polished. All this will be done twice more today, after lunch and before dinner. The barman checks his stock and polishes the already highly polished bar. Today's papers and all the glossy magazines are stacked and folded, should any guest wish to read them while waiting for his or her companion.

Down in the kitchen, porters briskly scrub the tiled floor, sweeping the water out through special drains dotted around the kitchen. Four more porters begin polishing hundreds of pieces of silver cutlery, each one with the specially designed Le Gavroche insignia of the little urchin on the handle. One porter does nothing but polish wine glasses, checking each one for the slightest smudge or imperfection.

The Wedgwood plates, also with the restaurant motif, are carefully stacked in the warming drawers under the pass, the control centre of the restaurant. This is where Michel Jr stands throughout each service, calling out the orders to the waiting chefs, and checking each dish to make sure it is perfect before he allows the waiters to take it through the glass doors into the restaurant.

OPPOSITE: Front of house preparations, making sure all is spotless in the dining room.

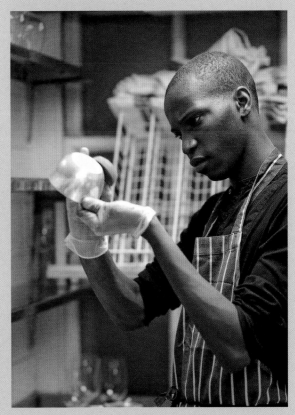

11am:

Silvano Giraldin, regarded without any argument at all as the best maître d' in London, circles the plush green and claret dining room, checking and checking again. He straightens one of the Joan Miró prints as he walks past. Silvano has been at Le Gavroche for nearly 40 years. He could spot a speck on a glass from 50 paces and knows everybody from Margaret Thatcher to Jon Bon Jovi. Oh, the stories he could tell about London society. But not today. And really, not ever. He walks from table to table as the waiters finish laying the tables. Each starched linen napkin is placed at just the right angle. Each glass is exactly the same distance from its neighbour and each red upholstered dining chair is perfectly aligned. On each table is placed one of the myriad fantastic sculptures created by the French artist Gérard Bouvier.

Silvano examines the sprays of mimosa, eucalyptus and lilies arranged in glazed urns in the restaurant and the luscious, oversized phalaenopsis orchids in the upstairs lounge. The 22 waiters and waitresses, mostly French but with some Americans and English among them, change into their black uniforms. They've already eaten lunch – guinea fowl, freshly made pasta and salad. It's one of the perks of the job. They work hard, but not many people get to dine at Le Gavroche every day.

Around 11.30, Michel Jr, Silvano and the senior staff have lunch. Being French, they do not allow this to be a casual or slapdash affair. They sit down at a corner table in the restaurant, eat their guinea fowl and salad, and talk. Silvano recalls the urbane gentleman who lunched here every day for 18 years, and another who travelled into London by train from his house in the country for his weekly treat, arriving promptly at 11.45 every Monday for 20 years. He and Michel Jr also remember with affection another guest who had dental problems, and so always ordered 'soft food'.

The tables are laid and all is nearly ready. Silvano gives his morning briefing, then some staff take a quick break before the rush.

12noon:

Lunch service is about to begin. The dining room has just been vacuumed again. The waiters check their black suits, smooth their hair, swallow the last of their coffee. Silvano has already briefed them on the day's specials.

Michel Jr is back in the kitchen, tasting and checking, always checking. 'A tiny bit more salt for the spinach mousse,' he says as he strides through to the fish section. Is each piece of sea bass a perfect diamond shape? Yes, chef. Is each scallop gleaming clean and standing ready to be poached? Yes, chef.

Then it's back to the meat section. The rabbit is braising. Good. Perfect rounds of fillet steak are stacked ready for roasting. OK. Over to the pastry section. The mille-feuilles are honey brown, crisp and flaky with a warm sweet aroma. The ice cream is out of the churn and in the freezer. All is ready.

Michel Jr is back at the pass, ready for lunch. Above his head are the bright warming lights and above them are three shelves holding those wonderful silver domes with their individual emblems. To the side is water for him to drink during service, small bowls of finely chopped herbs for garnishes, and a cloth to wipe the edges of any plate that is less than perfect. Everything and everyone is ready. The service begins.

OPPOSITE: Things are really hotting up now. Michel advises on the macaroons and constantly checks and tastes what is being prepared.

1pm

 The doors from the kitchen into the restaurant swing open almost every 30 seconds. The dining room is full. There is a backwash of quiet conversation – social and political gossip, the stock market, and what is on the day's menu. Silvano is everywhere, smiling, unhurried, but completely in control. Although Michel Jr dispensed with the regulation about men wearing ties some years ago, most males still wear one. The sommelier helps diners to choose wine from the 65,000 bottles in the cellar.

Inside the kitchen, orders are pegged on one side of the pass and Michel Jr calls them out the minute they come in. 'Two scallops. Four poached eggs on cod brandade.'

'Three rabbit... one beef, medium... three lobsters.' Each chef calls back, 'Yes, chef'.

There is no panic, no histrionics, but the pressure is palpable and Michel Jr has only one thing on his mind – a perfect plate of food. The prawn and avocado canapé given to all diners has to be right in the centre of the plate. The foie gras terrine has to have just the right amount of truffle vinaigrette, not a drop more or less. And as plate after plate leaves the pass, Michel is still calling back to his team, 'Make sure the water has salt in it... Is that beef under the grill... I want the cod cheek in two minutes. Sea bass in five... Can you hear me?' Back comes the reply, 'Yes, chef.'

In just over a minute, Michel Jr inspects, garnishes and sauces four different dishes. In less than two minutes, the waiters are placing them on tables in the restaurant. For more than an hour there is hardly a second's respite in this frenetic pace. The kitchen doors are on perpetual swinging motion. Everyone, from the porters scrubbing the pots and loading the dishwashers, to the sous-chefs cooking ten pieces of beef fillet to five different tastes, concentrates completely on their tasks. The kitchen staff love a joke, but never during service.

Nothing escapes Michel's attention. He takes every opportunity to teach his staff and improve their skills.

2pm:

Nearly all the main courses have been served. Some early arrivals have slipped away, but the restaurant is still almost full when Michel goes into the restaurant to greet his diners. 'I'm not a particularly gregarious person,' he says back in the kitchen. 'But it is good to show my face and keep in touch with the customers. And today was good... sometimes almost the whole restaurant wants the fixed-price menu, but today for some reason, there were a lot of orders from the à la carte. It makes a change.'

He makes himself a coffee from the espresso machine, takes a sip and gets back to work. While the chefs from the main kitchen are busy scrubbing and cleaning their preparation areas and their stoves, the pastry chefs are bringing their dishes to the pass – delicate creations of fresh fruit and cream on bases of paper-thin pastry dusted with icing sugar. The plates are whisked away into the dining room. The ice cream and sorbets have been transferred before lunch into a special trolley inside the restaurant and are served by the waiters.

Lunch is nearly over at Le Gavroche. But for those who can manage it, trays of petits fours, artfully arranged with chocolates and lace-thin biscuits, are served with coffee or tea. Guests linger over these for as long as they like. There is never any hurry in the restaurant, only in the kitchen.

3pm:

The restaurant is empty now. The last diner, happily replete, has just walked up the stairs, and out into Upper Brook Street. As the receptionist closes the door behind him, the cleaners start again. They vacuum, they dust, they plump and they polish upstairs and downstairs. The tables, already cleared, are stripped of their fine linens and relaid for dinner.

In the kitchen, the floor is scrubbed and sluiced again and every surface is wiped down. Everything is tidied. The bins are emptied. Michel Jr slips away for a run in Battersea Park, but only after

ensuring everything is ready and in order for dinner tonight and the next day's business. Most of the porters and chefs relax in the staff dining room, but others keep working. They check the supplies in the three walk-in larders and return telephone calls they were too busy to take during service. Then, and only then, will they get a chance to take a break.

4pm:

Sshh. For the first and only time in the day, Le Gavroche is quiet.

5pm:

Michel Jr is back from his run. The kitchen is full and busy. The waiters are about to change their uniforms for dinner. They've already eaten – this time couscous and roast pork with vegetables.

Silvano briefs the staff on the evening ahead, a private dinner for 100 guests. The hosts have decided on extraordinarily fine wines, among them a 2000 Y d'Yquem, a dry wine made from equal parts of Sémillon and Sauvignon Blanc grapes. It is so rare that it is not produced each year. There is also a 1989 and a 1999 Château Cheval Blanc, one of the finest wines from the St Emilion district, as well as 1989, 1983 and 1981 Château D'Yquem to accompany the dessert. Michel Jr has devised an equally fine menu – a ragout of langoustines and scallops, followed by foie gras, then milk-fed lamb from the Pyrenees and finally pear mille-feuille with caramel sauce.

In the twilight, the restaurant dining room looks even more glamorous and exotic. There are glasses in four different sizes in front of each place setting. Silvano moves around the room for his final inspection. Some things are not quite as he wants them. Immediately they are corrected.

6pm:

The kitchen floor is scrubbed and sluiced again. Trays of langoustines and scallops are ready for their final poaching. Lobes of foie gras stand waiting to be grilled. In the vegetable preparation area parsnips and carrots are sliced with surgical precision, each one exactly the same as the one before it. Potatoes are shaped into perfect rounds.

The meat chefs have already browned the boned legs of lamb and they sit ready for the oven. Beside them are the racks of lamb. Each guest will be served a slice of leg of lamb as well as a rack so they can savour the deeper richer flavour of the leg with the more delicate and tender meat on the bone. And then there will be the perfectly ripe Roquefort and Fourme D'Ambert, one of the oldest and mildest French blue cheeses, followed by the sumptuous pear mille-feuille.

Everything is ready. The plates are in the warming drawer under the pass. The warming lights are on. Silvano gives last-minute instructions to the waiters and Michel dons a fresh white jacket.

7pm:

The first of the 100 guests gather upstairs. With their 1995 Taittinger, they are served delicious canapés – miniature diamonds of pissaladière, rillettes of pork on toast, mouthfuls of lobster salad served on antique silver spoons, and warm pastilla of pigeon. One by one the silver trays leave the kitchen full and return minutes later, empty except for the intricately carved vegetable decorations. The pace quickens and then the door swings open. Michel Jr's father, Albert, is a guest at the party. Father and son hug and Albert greets some of the staff who worked under him until he handed over the running of the restaurant to his son in 1991. He's dapper and immaculate, right down to his highly polished crocodile-skin shoes.

The waiters take the bread baskets and the pots of salted and unsalted butter to each table. Silvano comes into the kitchen, 'Five minutes, chef. We go ahead in five minutes.' Michel takes his place at the pass. His glass of water, his garnishes and sauces are ready.

CLOCKWISE FROM TOP LEFT: Michel talking over the plan of action for the evening with his head chef and sous-chef. Emmanuel, who has taken over as manager following Silvano's retirement in 2008. Kitchen staff hard at work. Stocks and sauces ready and waiting.

8pm:

The hum of conversation from the restaurant is clearly audible now. Silvano, stern as any general, marshals his staff. 'Do as I say. Go when I tell you.' No one would dare disobey him. He nods at Michel and the order to start goes back into the kitchen. And here it comes. Plates of langoustine and scallops are placed on the pass. Michel inspects, garnishes and drizzles just the right amount of sauce on each one. Waiters hover by the door waiting for Silvano's command. When it comes, they queue to pick up a plate, turn around and then launch themselves through the doors.

Ten people on table eight? Michel and Silvano know without being told. Four people on table six? They know that too. Somehow both men know how many people are sitting at each table in the restaurant. And so each diner at every table is served at exactly the same moment as the others and within five minutes all 100 guests are contemplating some of the best shellfish available in England prepared by some of the best cooks in the country.

The courses roll out in orchestrated perfection. After the fish comes the sizzling foie gras with raisin confit. The aroma would make angels faint. The plates return to the kitchen scraped clean. The porters load the dishwashers again and again. Everyone in this kitchen is working as hard as they can. Now it is time for the lamb, cooked to a perfect rosy pink, served with baby vegetables and fondant potatoes. Again, Silvano choreographs his staff. They leave and enter the kitchen as precisely as any corps de ballet.

OPPOSITE: Michel at the pass, checking the orders and everything that goes out into the dining room.

9pm:

Michel Jr stands up straight for the first time in an hour and walks around the kitchen, chatting to the staff. Everyone looks relieved and pleased. The pressure, for tonight at least, is over. But not the work. Every surface has to be scrubbed clean and wiped down again. Once again the buckets and scrubbing brushes come out and the floor is washed down. The antique silver spoons used to serve the lobster salad canapés are washed, polished and stored away.

After this brief lull, it is time for the cheese course, and out it goes, served with wafer-thin sourdough toast, celery and quince jam. Again, the plates come back empty and Michel allows himself a smile. For any cook, even one with two Michelin stars, a plate scraped clean is the best compliment of all. He goes out into the restaurant and the applause from the diners rings through to the back of the kitchen. He is tired. Apart from a short break, he has been working for more than 13 hours.

10pm:

The dessert plates are spread out all over the preparation areas. First, the caramel sauce is carefully ladled on each one, then the pastry cooks place a feather light mille-feuille, with its fresh pear and sabayon filling, in the exact centre of each plate. A light dusting of icing sugar, followed by a sprinkling of crushed pistachio nuts and these are ready to be served. Out they go into the restaurant, each one an edible still-life.

The waiters stand by to prepare coffee and tisanes, and serve the trays of petits fours. After a final inspection, Michel Jr's work is over for the night. Silvano, ever the general, directs his staff in and out of the restaurant with his inimitable military precision. Everyone moves quickly and efficiently, but they are more relaxed than at any other time in the evening. One hundred people have enjoyed what is probably the culinary experience of their lives. For Le Gavroche and its staff, it is the end of just another day.

OPPOSITE: A quote from Brillat-Savarin's famous work 'Physiologie du goût' (The Physiology of Taste), which was published in 1825. In the book Brillat-Savarin, noted epicure and gourmet, expounds on the pleasures of the table.

Le plaisir de la table
est de tous les âges,
de toutes les conditions,
de tous les pays et de tous les jours;
il peut s'associer
à tous les autres plaisirs
et reste le dernier pour nous
consoler de leur perte.

BRILLAT-SAVARIN
Physiologie du Goût

Pour Monsieur Rouse

Toutes Mes Amitiées Gourmandes

Beaune 29 Avril 1994

The basics

All great food starts with the best and freshest ingredients, and this includes really good stock. Especially in French cuisine, stocks are the building blocks of fine sauces, soups, stews and many other dishes. The stocks can be made in advance and then frozen into convenient smaller batches. They can also be reduced down to a glaze and then frozen in an ice-cube tray. These can then be used as a concentrate, rather like your own home-made stock cubes but with a far superior flavour and giving much better results.

My pastry apprenticeship taught me the skills and appreciation of the basics that are needed to achieve not only the classics but also the more contemporary desserts.

The following are all recipes you will need to complete some of the dishes in this book, but they are also basic skills you need to master and that will vastly improve your life in the kitchen.

VEAL STOCK

MAKES ABOUT 3.5 LITRES
1.5kg veal knuckle bones, chopped
1 calf's foot, split
1 large onion, roughly chopped
2 large carrots, roughly chopped
1 stick of celery, roughly chopped
5 litres water
2 cloves of garlic
2 sprigs of thyme
½ tablespoon tomato purée

Roast the bones and calf's foot in a hot oven (220°C/Gas 7), turning them occasionally until they are brown all over, then put them into a large saucepan.

Put the onion, carrots and celery into the roasting pan and roast until golden, turning frequently with a wooden spatula. Pour off any excess fat and put the roasted vegetables into the pan with the bones.

Put the roasting pan over high heat and add 500ml of the water to deglaze the pan; scrape the bottom with a wooden spoon to loosen all the caramelised sugars, then pour into the saucepan with the bones.

Add the remaining ingredients and bring to the boil. Skim off the scum and fat that come to the surface. Turn down the heat and simmer gently for 3 hours or so, skimming occasionally. Pass through a fine sieve and leave to cool. This can be kept in the refrigerator for 8–10 days, or frozen.

VEGETABLE STOCK

1 leek
1 carrot
1 onion
1 clove garlic
1 bay leaf
1 sprig thyme

Wash, peel and chop the vegetables, cover with cold water
and simmer for 20 minutes.

WHITE CHICKEN STOCK

MAKES ABOUT 4 LITRES

2kg chicken bones or wing tips
1 calf's foot, split
5 litres water
1 onion
1 small leek
2 sticks of celery
2 sprigs of thyme
6 parsley stalks

Place the bones and calf's foot in a large saucepan, cover with the
water and bring to the boil. Once the stock is boiling, skim off the
scum and fat that come to the surface. Turn the heat down, add
the remaining ingredients and simmer for 1½ hours, skimming
occasionally. Pass the stock through a fine sieve and leave to cool.
This can be kept in the refrigerator for up to 5 days, or frozen.

BROWN CHICKEN STOCK

MAKES ABOUT 5 LITRES
2kg chicken bones or wing tips
1 calf's foot, split
olive oil
1 onion
1 carrot
1 stick celery
5 cloves garlic
1 tablespoon tomato paste
2 sprigs thyme

Drizzle the bones and calf's foot with olive oil and roast at 220°C/ Gas 7 until brown. Place the bones in a deep saucepan, cover with about 5 litres of cold water and bring to a gentle simmer.

Meanwhile, place the roasting tray on the hob, add the peeled and chopped vegetables and garlic, and then fry until golden. Add the tomato puree, thyme and about a litre of water. Stir well to remove any bits stuck to the roasting tray. Once boiling, pour all the contents into the pan and continue to simmer for 2 hours, skimming when necessary. Pass through a fine sieve and chill.

DUCK JUS

MAKES ABOUT 1.25 LITRES
1kg duck bones, chopped and
   excess fat removed
3 shallots, sliced
100ml port
1.5 litres white chicken stock

Roast the bones in a hot oven (220°C/Gas 7) until browned, then drain
off the excess fat and put the bones in a deep saucepan. Brown the
shallots in the roasting pan, stirring frequently. Pour in the port and
stir with a spatula to loosen the caramelised residue. Boil to reduce
by half, then pour over the bones. Add the stock and bring to the
boil. Simmer for 45 minutes, then strain.

SWEET MADEIRA SAUCE

MAKES ABOUT 500ML
3 shallots, peeled and sliced
2 tablespoons butter
10 button mushrooms
1 bottle sweet Madeira

2 litres veal stock (see p. 303)
100ml truffle juice
salt and pepper
chopped truffle (optional)

Cook the shallots in a large pan with a knob of butter over a medium
heat until golden-brown. Add the sliced mushrooms and continue to
cook until tender. Pour in the Madeira and boil until reduced by half.
Add the stock and truffle juice, reduce by two-thirds, and then pass
through a fine sieve. Check seasoning and whisk in a little butter
and chopped truffle if using.

COURT BOUILLON

MAKES ABOUT 2.25 LITRES

2 carrots
white part of 1 leek
1 stick celery
½ fennel bulb
4 shallots
2 small white onions
1.5 litres water
750ml dry white wine
2 tablespoons white wine vinegar
1 bouquet garni
25g coarse sea salt
1 tablespoon cracked black
   or white peppercorns

Peel the carrots, leek, celery, fennel, shallots and onions, then slice into thin (3mm) rounds.

Bring the water, wine and vinegar to the boil and add all the vegetables, bouquet garni and salt, and the peppercorns tied in a little muslin bag. Simmer for 15 minutes, until the vegetables are cooked, but still a little crunchy. Strain and chill.

This can be kept in the fridge for 3–4 days. The vegetables can be used as part of a recipe.

CRÈME ANGLAISE

MAKES 750ML

500ml milk
1 vanilla pod, split
6 egg yolks
120g caster sugar

Bring the milk to the boil with the vanilla pod. Remove the pan from the heat, cover and leave to infuse for 10 minutes.

Beat the egg yolks with the sugar until thick and creamy. Bring the milk back to the boil and pour on to the yolk mixture, whisking continuously. Pour the mixture back into the saucepan and cook over low heat, stirring continuously with a spatula, until the custard thickens slightly.

VANILLA SUGAR

For vanilla sugar, take one vanilla pod, split it and place it in 500g of granulated sugar. Cover tightly and leave for a couple of days. Then put the sugar and vanilla pod into a food processor and blitz until the vanilla pod has powdered. You should now have a fine, greyish-looking sugar with black specks. This sugar keeps for months in an airtight container.

BASIC SPONGE

6 eggs, separated
190g caster sugar
180g plain flour
icing sugar for dusting

Preheat the oven to 220°C/Gas 7. Whisk the egg yolks with two-thirds of the caster sugar until the mixture is pale and has a ribbon consistency. In a clean bowl, whisk the egg whites until risen, add the remaining caster sugar and continue to whisk until firm. Fold about one-third of the whites into the yolk mixture with a slotted spoon. When fully mixed, add the rest of the whites and gently fold them in. When the whites are almost incorporated, add the flour and gently mix in. Keep the mixture very light and airy and don't over-mix.

Pipe strips of the mixture, 10 x 2cm, on to a baking mat, dust with icing sugar and bake in the hot oven for 8 minutes. Leave to cool a little before lifting onto a wire rack.

Index

Entries in **bold** refer to recipes

Acknowledgements

Thanks to Suellen Dainty and her tape recorder for putting my chef parlance into written words; to the ever-present Marion, the only person that can break the code of my handwriting; Susan, Jinny, Lucie and all the team at Orion for their expertise and professionalism; Alex, Emma and Fontaine at Smith & Gilmour for their design; Peter Horridge for his calligraphy. And thanks to Cristian Barnett for his glorious food and action shots.

Thanks, too, to my sous-chef Chris 'the Spick' for cooking all the food for the photography; and to Rachel, the first female head chef at the helm of Le Gavroche. Without her I would not have time to do anything else other than cook. Last but not least, thanks to every member of the Roux clan – you have shaped and inspired me over the years.

PHOTOGRAPH CREDITS
Food and Le Gavroche kitchens: Cristian Barnett
15 left: Country Life magazine
130: Bernard Vaussion
222: Gemma Levigne
Cover, 38, 223, 297 (top right): Jon Wyand

Other photographs from the Roux family albums